Rafi Fernandez (née Tayabally) was born in Secunderabad, India, in 1944 and has lived in England since 1965. Although a science graduate, she did a secretarial course in order to qualify for a UK work permit and to join her boyfriend, whom she then married in 1968. They had been pen friends since she was twelve and had met when she was sixteen, but owing to their different religions, they were only allowed to marry in England.

Having worked in a travel agency and for Air-India, Rafi Fernandez has travelled throughout the world and it was this which led to her interest in cooking for pleasure. She attended the Culinary Techniques Workshop at the Carrier Seminar of Cooking and in 1983 she started to organize her own catering events, 'West Meets East Through Food'. She is also the author of *Malaysian Cookery* (1985).

Rafi Fernandez

Indian
Vegetarian
Cookery

I dedicate this book to my mother with a prayer: O Lord, reward her for bringing me up and recompense her for loving me and guard her as she guarded me.

This edition published 1996 by Diamond Books
77-85 Fulham Palace Road
Hammersmith
London W6 8JB

First published 1986 by Fontana Paperbacks

Contents

Acknowledgements

I would like to thank Air-India, London, for their invaluable assistance without which my tour of India would not have been possible.

I would also like to thank everyone in India who so generously shared their recipe secrets with me.

Preface

I tried many of the recipes in this book for the first time in 1984 when I spent ten weeks touring India. I collected them from members of my family, friends, servants, new acquaintances, and even some from restaurants. Although I was born in India and lived there until I was twenty-one years old, I did not really pay any attention to the cuisine. I was satisfied by what appeared on our dining table. Between 1965, when I first arrived in the UK, and 1980, I cooked because it was part of my duty as a housewife and a mother. In 1980, when I resigned from my full-time job in London and moved to a tiny rural village on the borders of Essex and Suffolk, I realized that I had a lot of spare time on my hands. I found to my surprise that I had an in-built talent for artistic cooking and ventured further afield from the basic cooking I had been doing until then. In 1983 I decided I could never be just an ordinary housewife and, with my sons away at school all day, I needed a part-time occupation which would still allow me time with them but would provide me with an outside interest. At this point I took up preparing oriental meals at local village pubs, and the once-a-month events became so popular that I began to expand my repertoire.

Traditional dishes were available at restaurants so I had to formulate new ideas: often I produced dishes which were entirely my own invention but they always seemed to work. So, when I was writing this book I did not want to cramp it with dishes which have often appeared in other recipe books. However, to put together enough original recipes I knew I would have to return to my motherland because, like so many people who live in any country for a long time, I had taken India for granted during the years I had lived there. The 1984 visit opened my eyes. With vegetarian cuisine in mind, I toured the entire country, picking up wonderful ideas from all kinds of people. On my return I tried out all their ideas, and the recipes in this book are the result. I ate only vegetarian food during my ten-week visit to enable me to concentrate on how each region prepared the same selection of vegetables, pulses, cereals and fruits in a different way. The difference was usually just in the addition or omission of perhaps one spice or herb.

When you read the recipes you may feel in some cases that the amounts given for ingredients are too large. But throughout the book the same spices and herbs are used in different combinations and proportions and once you start stocking your larder it will not seem so confusing. All the dry spices store indefinitely in airtight jars and there are useful hints in Basic Ingredients (pages 14–47) on how to store fresh herbs. I have also experimented carefully with vegetables which I cannot readily obtain in a rural village and have given you freezing suggestions for these.

Although non-vegetarians in India are very particular about meat, poultry and fish, it is interesting to note that a housewife selects only one of these three for a daily meal but produces three or four, sometimes even five, vegetarian dishes on the table. One wonders why. Since I have taken up cooking as a profession, I have been disturbed by remarks like 'vegetarian food is only fit for rabbits' or 'it's poor man's fare'. This is sad because vegetables do not lack any of the nutritional values our bodies require and in some cases contain more.

Since my tour of India my husband and sons were subjected to vegetarian menus while I tested the recipes I had brought back with me. Initially there were grumbles, but as the year went by they were thoroughly enjoying themselves. When all the tests were finally completed I expected a sigh of relief from them. Not so . . . My husband, who enjoys a good meal, was very appreciative and was often amazed by my accomplishments. My son Kevin, who loves his meat, paid me a great compliment by saying that he was astounded by how varied and how delicious my vegetarian menus were throughout the year, and my other son, Lee, has become a full-time

Preface

vegetarian. If, therefore, I was able to provide a different menu each day using vegetables, cereals, pulses and fruits, my book will, I promise, enable you to do the same.

Rafi Fernandez
Belchamp Walter, 1985

Introduction

India covers 1,261,813 square miles, with a population of over 700,000,000, and is steeped in culture and customs which are thousands of years old. For hundreds of years India was under foreign rule but this did not influence the cuisine. Even today dishes are prepared from recipes which have been passed down the generations by word of mouth. The majority of Indians are Hindu and therefore mainly vegetarian. Economic and climatic conditions also account for the large percentage of vegetarians. Many people in India still practise *ahimsa*, a teaching of non-violence to any living thing. Ghandiji, father of the Indian nation, once answered a journalist thus:

The secret of good life?
A clear heart and conscience,
A cool head and regular communion with God,
Abstention from carnal food and pleasure,
No alcohol, smoking and condiments,
A very strict vegetarian diet,
And love for all my fellow men.

In the beginning man was purely vegetarian. The Holy Bible tells (and it was later narrated in the Holy Quran) that God created the world in six days and rested on the seventh. At the end of that week He gave for food fruits, grains and nuts and later vegetables and herbs were added. On this diet man lived and many counted their life span in hundreds of years. Wickedness came to man and God punished him with a universal flood. Eight persons survived on an ark built by Noah and when the floods subsided they found themselves on the high mountains of Ararat. With no plant life available, God

11

gave man permission to eat meat and research studies have found that since that time the span of man's life was shortened.

In the Preface I talked about my ten-week tour of India. This was done on a limited budget of £5 a day which included hotels, meals and transport (excluding air fares). Most hotels we stayed in were simple, clean and practical and usually cost about £1 per night. Meals also were eaten at humble restaurants and these amazed even me. The meals were simply served but were very appetizing and most restaurateurs were always ready to share their recipe secrets with me.

In Agra, which was the hottest day of our tour, we popped into a 5-star hotel to cool off and I chose a fruit salad which was priced Rs.20 (just over £1). To my horror a tiny bowl of tinned fruit was placed before me. Two days later in Khajuraho we stayed in a tiny hotel and for breakfast I had *idlis* with *sambhar* for Rs.2.50 (approximately 15p) and a fruit salad priced at Rs.5 (30p). While waiting for the fruit salad I noticed a young lad being sent off to the open market which was across the road and when the salad reached my table it was beautifully displayed with fresh banana, sweet-lime, orange, guava and papaya. After that we went to 5-star hotels only to cool off with a beer or fruit juice. Many days we only took snacks at roadside stalls. India loves titbits and the variety and range are so immense that it was a hard task to select my favourite ones to include in this book.

In total we visited twenty-one cities or towns and, depending on the form of transport available in each place, we made friends with rickshaw men, autorickshaw drivers, taxi drivers and so on. They were very helpful and took us to places we would never have found on our own. In Varanasi, a city throbbing with religion, we journeyed by boat down the River Ganges to see the famous *ghats* (steps) on the riverbank. It was monsoon time and the tides were high. We visited several temples where we ate *prasadams* – food prepared in honour of presiding deities and given free to pilgrims. Most *prasadams* are milk-based sweets. Milk is boiled down and mixed with sugar and a variety of ingredients like rice, lentils, vegetables, fruits and nuts. In the north these are called *kheer* and in the south *payasams*. The Muslims make *kheer* with rice and in my home in India this is served with *puris* – deep-fried un-leavened bread. A room is specially cleaned for the occasion and the cooking and serving must take place within it. Only Muslims can enter the room wearing clean clothes and having first bathed. A member of the family reads a story about a woodcutter's wife who took a vow that if her husband brought home enough money to feed the family for a few days she would prepare a feast in the name of Bibi Mariam – a saint like Lady Fatima – and feed her other poor friends. Her husband found treasure buried in a dead tree and they became very rich. She kept her promise and each year on that day a meal of *kheer* and *puris* is prepared. Earthen pots are used around which raw lentils, rice, mint, flowers and fresh vegetables are decoratively placed. The food is shared among the poor and the decorative grains and vegetables given to them to use in their cooking. I don't know when this custom came about but as a child I remember the girls in our family would hunt for delicate silver rings that were put into the *kheer*, for, if one was found, it was a sign of good luck and they were worn on the fingers of the right hand only.

I have included recipes which are traditionally Bhori – a small Muslim community to which I belong. This community originated from Surat, north of Bombay, and I do not think any one outside the community has published these recipes before. In India Bhori meals are well known. We start and finish our meals with a sweet dish, in between which there are five or six savoury dishes.

India is steeped in folklore, and tales that have been narrated for generations often involve particular dishes or ingredients. While I was in the state of Maharashtra I heard a delightful story. A king was once ill with a carbuncle on his back. No one could cure him. One day, while resting in the forest, he met a poor shepherd. The shepherd loved his king dearly and, seeing him in pain, prepared a paste of herbs which he said would cure the king's illness. The king accepted the paste and promised that if he was cured he would give the shepherd anything he asked for. The king was cured in a few days and sent for the shepherd so that he might keep his promise. The shepherd was delighted to see his king recovered but all he asked for was a blanket to keep him warm. Not only stories like these but also tests have shown that Indian herbs and spices have remedial values as well as titillating flavours.

This book has been compiled not just for vegetarians but also in the hope that it will provide non-vegetarians with new ideas and scope. Perhaps the wide range of recipes in this book may even convert some non-vegetarians to vegetarian food, particularly those who consider it to be 'rabbit food' or 'poor man's fare'.

Basic Ingredients

When I first began reading cookery books I ignored the early chapters and moved straight on to the recipes. As a result, I often found that I didn't understand some of the methods. So study with me now the basic ingredients which have been used in this book. Not only do they provide nutrition; many of them also help to beautify a person, for it must be appreciated that commercial cosmetics were introduced to India not very long ago. How, therefore, have we Indians always been such a beautiful race (if I may say so myself)? Read on and find out.

I have given the ingredients in English, Hindi, Gujerati, Urdu and Tamil which I hope will help you when shopping. For ethnic readers I hope it brings back pleasant memories of home.

ABBREVIATIONS

H	Hindi	G	Gujerati
U	Urdu	T	Tamil

Basic Ingredients

GREEN LEAFY VEGETABLES

In India we are blessed with a wealth of green leafy vegetables, an excellent source of vitamins and minerals, and a minimum of 115g (4½ oz) per person should be included in the daily diet. Some of the more popular varieties are fenugreek (*methi*), spinach (*palak*), amaranth (*chaulia*), dill (*soova*) rosella (*ambat*), drumstick leaves (*segava*) and red sorrell (*chukkay*). The protein content of green leafy vegetables, although only present in small amounts, is also valuable, and when mixed with lentils and cereals the nutritive quality of the food improves considerably. Many Indian leafy vegetables can now be found in Indian grocery shops but if they are not readily available, use tender leaves from vegetables like carrot, beetroot, colcasia, turnip and radish.

Brussels Sprouts
H/U: *Chote bund gobhi*   G: *Nhanu kobi*   T: *Kalakose*

Brussels sprouts are not readily available in India but are very high in vitamins and potassium and I find they are delicious when spiced. You can substitute brussels sprouts for any cabbage recipe.

To freeze: Choose tender heads. Discard outer leaves if they are discoloured. Blanch for 3–4 minutes and cool in iced water. Open freeze and then pack in polythene bags. Cook from frozen.

Cabbage
H/U: *Bund gobhi*   G: *Kobi*   T: *Muttaikosu*

Cabbage is extremely rich in vitamins and potassium. However, too much overcooked cabbage is harmful and this can be rectified by adding a pinch of asafoetida (see page 29) while cooking. One cup of fresh cabbage juice taken with a teaspoon of honey daily has been used in India from ancient times for several ailments, including helping poor sight in darkness.

To freeze: Blanch shredded leaves for 1½ minutes then follow

15

the same method as for brussels sprouts (above). Cook from frozen.

Carrot Leaves
H/U: *Gajar sag*   G: *Gajjar pan*   T: *Mangal kosu*

Carrot leaves are usually discarded, but God has provided us with a very valuable nutritional treasure here. Tender leaves can be used as a substitute for ordinary spinach and raw in a green salad. A glass of fresh leaf-juice with a pinch of salt and a teaspoon of lime juice not only supplies all the daily requirements of vitamins, but tones the digestive system, and strengthens eyes, lungs, heart and liver. Juice with a pinch of turmeric is used in India to massage the face to cure pimples and blackheads.
To freeze: Blanch leaves and tender stems for 1½ minutes. Cool completely in iced water, drain and pack in polythene bags and freeze. To use, thaw and cook but reduce cooking time.

Fenugreek
H/U: *Methi sag*   G: *Methi bhaji*   T: *Vendhayam kerai*

Fenugreek is a very popular leafy vegetable cultivated all over India. It is used in both vegetarian and non-vegetarian dishes. Although it has a slightly bitter taste, this vegetable has remained popular through folklore medicine. Fresh leaves are applied to the scalp to cure dandruff, and paste is applied to breasts to stop the secretion of milk. Fenugreek can be easily grown in a greenhouse, and should be picked when the first two leaves appear.
To freeze: See method for carrot leaves (above).

Lettuce
H/U: *Kahu* or *kasmi sag*   G: *Salat*   T: *Aver kerai*

In India this is popular as a cooked vegetable and also raw in salads. It is very good for you during pregnancy. It is said that in the olden days lettuce was fed to an ass and a cupful of its milk was given daily to pregnant girls.

Spinach
H/U: *Palak sag*   G: *Palak bhaji*   T: *Passale kerai*

Spinach leaves are very cooling and nutritious, and are one of the cheapest vegetables that supply the same amount of protein as an equal quantity of eggs, meat, fish or chicken. It is also a very useful addition to children's diet.

To freeze: Blanch leaves and tender stems for 1½–2 minutes. Cool thoroughly in iced water and drain. Pack portions in polythene bags and freeze. To use, thaw, drain excess water and cook for a shorter length of time.

NON-LEAFY VEGETABLES

Non-leafy vegetables are most used as bulk food after grains and cereals. Chiefly consisting of the fruit, roots and tubers of various plants, they are cheap to buy, supply minerals and vitamins, and contain plenty of cellulose.

Bitter Gourd
H/U/G: *Karela*   T: *Pavakkai*

A very popular fruit vegetable cultivated all over India which has been specially used as a folk medicine for diabetes since ancient times. There are two varieties: the larger kind is oblong and pale green in colour while the other is oval and dark green. Both types are bitter in taste and turn reddish-orange when they ripen.

To freeze: Scrape and cut into pieces. Remove any pith and seeds. Soak in salted water for 1 hour. Drain. Blanch for 2 minutes and cool in iced water. Open freeze before packing in polythene bags. Alternatively, stir-fry for 2 minutes after soaking and open freeze before packing.

Bottle Gourd
H/U: *Lawki* or *lamba kaddu*   G: *Dudhi*   T: *Churaikai*

Extensively cultivated in India. The fruit is yellowish green and shaped like a bottle, but should not be eaten raw. In the centre of the fruit there is a white spongy pulp with seeds. It is used mainly in vegetable and pulse dishes, and the peel, which is rich in potassium, can be used to make a snack (page 256). In India young maidens massage their bodies with the inner side of the peel to lighten their complexion.

To freeze: See method for bitter gourd (page 17).

Brinjal/Eggplant/Aubergine
H/U: *Baingan*   G: *Ringana* or *vaingan*   T: *Katterikaya*

This shiny purple-coloured fruit which is now so popular all over the world comes from a plant that is a native of India. It can easily be used as a substitute for meat as it is a wholesome bulk food. There are many varieties, one of which is round, light purple-white in colour, and resembles an egg. The most popular variety is dark purple. These are sometimes slender and long or fat and round. Most varieties have a soft pulpy inside with seeds. They are edible from the time they are a quarter grown until they are near ripe. Brinjals discolour very easily and should therefore be cut just before use, or soaked in cold water soon after they are cut. The water can be used later to wash hands and face for a fresh feel.

To freeze: Bring water to the boil. Cut the aubergine in pieces or slices and blanch for 4 minutes. Cool and open freeze before packing. Use from frozen.

Broad Beans/Double Beans
H/U: *Kalisiam-ki-phalli/chastny*   G: *Fafda papdi/papdi*
T: *Karpu avaraikai*

Indian broad beans are not as long as those available in the West. They tend to be about five to seven centimetres (two to three inches) long. The pods are greenish purple in colour and have three or four dark purple seeds. This vegetable is very popular in the states of Maharashtra or Gujerat. It is sometimes combined with meat and you can include soya bean chunks to obtain a similar result.

To freeze: Cut or leave whole. Blanch for 2 minutes. Cool and open freeze before packing in polythene bags. Cook from frozen.

Capsicum/Green, Red or Yellow Pepper
H/U: *Simla mirch* or *badi mirch*   G: *Motamircha*
T: *Kodimilagai*

Popularly cooked in India with a meat or vegetable stuffing. Also eaten raw in salads.

To freeze: Wash, wipe and open freeze. To use, run under cold water and cut into desired shape while still frozen. Frozen peppers are not suitable for salads.

Cauliflower
H/U: *Phool gobhi*   G: *Pangoli* or *kobi phul*   T: *Kovippu*

Cauliflower plants belong to the cabbage and knol-knol family. Fresh and delicately cooked flowers are very nutritious. Cauliflower leaves should not be discarded as their vitamin A content is high. If you don't like the taste of the leaves boil them and drink the water like soup with a pinch of salt and pepper and a few drops of lime juice.

To freeze: Break into florets and cut the stem and leaves. Blanch florets and stems separately for 3 minutes. Blanch leaves for 2 minutes. Cool, pack separately and freeze. Frozen florets, stems and leaves can only be used in a curry.

Cluster Beans/Gipsy Beans
H/U: *Guvar phalli*   G: *Govar*   T: *Kothavarangai*

Cluster beans are widely grown all over India. They have a

slightly bitter taste but are delicious when cooked. Chewing one or two fresh cluster beans early in the morning prevents bad breath and cleans the tongue.
To freeze: See method for broad beans (page 18).

Cucumber
H/U: *Kakri/khira*   G: *Tansal* or *kakdi*
T: *Vellaripazham* or *kirakai*

Cucumber is mostly eaten raw in a salad or combined with buttermilk or natural yogurt. In India cucumber has to be prepared by cutting the ends and scrubbing the scum to remove any bitter taste. In the south of India a curry is also made (page 140). Grated cucumber spread over the face and neck is a natural face pack and an effective beauty aid.

Drumsticks/Moringa
H/U: *Sajjan ki phalli*   G: *Sargvani sing*   T: *Murangaikai*

A moringa tree is very beautiful and mostly grown in the backyard of most south Indian homes. The fruit, flowers and leaves are edible although only the fruit is sold in markets. The fruit is long and is cooked in India as a vegetable dish or combined with lentils.
To freeze: Scrape the outer skin and cut into 5-cm (2-inch) pieces. Blanch for 2–3 minutes and cool in iced water. Drain and open freeze before packing. Alternatively, stir-fry in a little oil for 2–3 minutes, cool, open freeze and pack.

French Beans
H/U: *Badi baquala* or *binnis*   G: *Fansa*   T: *Kulaka*

Beans are available throughout the year and cooked in various ways. They are ideal for those who require a low-calorie diet.
To freeze: See method for broad beans (page 18).

Gentlemen's Toes
H/U: *Tindla*   G: *Tindras*   T: *Quai*

These tender fruits are green and look like small cucumbers with white longitudinal stripes, but they become red when ripe. They can be used raw in salads and are very refreshing and nutritious.
To freeze: Stir-fry whole or halved in a little oil and open freeze before packing. Cook from frozen. Frozen *tindlas* cannot be used in salads.

Kholrabi/Knolkhol
H/U: *Gath gobhi*   G: *Nolkol*   T: *Knolkol*

Eaten cooked or raw, it is extremely rich in vitamin C. In India it is also made into a pickle (page 248).
To freeze: See method for cabbage (page 15). Frozen kholrabi cannot be used in salads or pickles.

Okra/Lady's Fingers or Gumbo
H/U: *Bhendi*   G: *Bhinda*   T: *Vendaikai*

One of the most common and popular vegetables grown all over India. The pods have a mucilage, which acts as a binder. Pulp of the pod is applied to the face to soften the skin and to cure pimples, and is also said to be a whitening beauty aid.
To freeze: Remove tops sparingly. Blanch whole for 1½–2 minutes. Cool in iced water. Open freeze before packing. Cook from frozen. Frozen okra should not be stir-fried on their own but can be used in a curry with gravy or in a lentil dish.

Peas
H: *Badla*   U: *Mattar*   G: *Vatana*   T: *Pattani podh*

In India fresh peas are very expensive so the dried varieties are more commonly used. Dried peas are roasted and sold cheaply by roadside hawkers as a common food item. They are one of India's most popular snacks (page 90) and are also combined in the 'Bombay Mix' which is now readily available in health-food shops and large supermarkets. Peas should not be eaten raw.

To freeze: Blanch for 1 minute and cool in iced water. Open freeze and pack. Cook from frozen.

Pumpkin

H: *Kumra*   U: *Lal kaddu*   G: *Lal phupala*
T: *Pushalni kumbul kaya*

A very popular fruit vegetable with an orange-coloured pulp. Used both in savoury and sweet culinary preparations. Cooked pumpkin is wholesome and ideal in a low-calorie diet.

To freeze: See method for bitter gourd (page 17).

Ridge Gourd

H/U: *Turai*   G: *Kadan* or *turiya*   T: *Peerkangkai*

A very delicious vegetable popular all over India. It is recommended in a diabetic diet and the soup made from this vegetable is nutritious for convalescents and children.

To freeze: See method for bitter gourd (page 17).

Snake Gourd

H/U: *Chichinda*   G: *Pandola*   T: *Pudalankai*

Very popular all over India, this is a snake-like, greyish white, spongy vegetable. Do not eat when overripe.

To freeze: See method for bitter gourd (page 17).

ROOTS AND TUBERS

Roots and tubers contain carbohydrates in the form of starch, but they are easily digestible compared to grains, cereals and pulses. Fresh vegetables belonging to this group also supply minerals, vitamins and fibre, and are cheap to buy.

Basic Ingredients

Beetroot

H/U: *Chugander*   G: *Beet*   T: *Beet*

In India beetroot is eaten as a salad and cooked in savoury and sweet dishes. Eating raw beet with honey is the cheapest source of vitamin C. The tender leaves are edible as a green leafy vegetable and, during the summer months when they are sold with the beetroot, can be substituted for spinach in any recipe.

To freeze: Cooked, peeled beetroot can be frozen without blanching. Thaw in the refrigerator and use in salads or curry. Frozen beetroot can be used to make *halwa* (page 258) if you grate it before freezing.

Carrots

H/U/G: *Gajjar*   G: *Mangal mullangi*

When I was a child my mother used to give me a cupful of carrot juice mixed with honey and cow's milk, together with ten almonds, every night and this was a natural mental tonic. Unani doctors in India insist that carrot *halwa* (see page 258) is a very effective tonic for people feeling weak. Chewing a carrot immediately after eating kills all the harmful germs in the mouth, cleans the teeth and removes food particles lodged in crevices.

To freeze: Cut large carrots into strips or dice. Leave small tender carrots whole. Blanch cut carrots for 3 minutes and whole carrots for 4–5 minutes. Cool in iced water and open freeze before packing. Use from frozen. Frozen carrots can be used to prepare *halwa* (see page 258) only if they have been grated before blanching and freezing.

Colocasia

H/U: *Arvi* or *kachalu*   G: *Alvi*   T: *Sepan kizhangu*

In folklore medicine this is used extensively as an aphrodisiac. It also increases body weight. Its leaves can be used as a green leafy vegetable instead of spinach.

Onion
H/U: *Piyaz*   G: *Dungli* or *kanda*   T: *Vengayam*

Onions are used very extensively all over the world without many people realizing their antiseptic effects. Onion is often mentioned in Indian folklore as a preventive medicine for many ailments. A few slices of onion with vinegar taken immediately after eating prevents tooth decay, indigestion and food poisoning. Onion leaves are very rich in vitamins so use them often in your cooking or chopped in salads.

Kajal (known as khol in the West) has been used by Indians for centuries for eye makeup but it also has medicinal properties for eyes. In India as soon as a baby's eyes are open *kajal* is applied to help the eyes, add beauty and as a mark to keep evil away. You can make *kajal* at home using the following method, which I remember as a young girl is how my *ayah* (maid) prepared it.

Soak a clean cloth in fresh white onion juice and dry it in the shade. Repeat this three times. Then soak the same cloth in fresh fennel-leaf juice and dry. Repeat this three times. Make a wick of the cloth and dip in pure castor oil. Light it and collect the soot over a copper plate. Scrape the soot and store in a glass jar after mixing in a little pure ghee. Use sparingly (and do not cry as it will spread).

Potato
H/U: *Aloo*   G: *Batata*   T: *Urulaikizhangu*

Next to wheat and rice, potato is extensively cultivated in India, since the Spanish sailors introduced it. It is a cheap, delicious bulk food, available in all seasons and able to be stored for a long time, which makes it very popular. Potato peel is very nutritious and it is therefore advisable to cook potatoes with their peel whenever possible. Potatoes have a pigment which alters the colour of the vegetable when cut. To avoid this, soak in water after they are cut or cut them just before use. Face unexpected guests with equanimity when you only have potatoes in the house. They are easily moulded into shapes,

Wheat
H/U: *Gehun*   G: *Ghau*   T: *Godumai*

Wholemeal flour   H/U: *Gehun atta*   G: *Ghau ato*
T: *Godumai mavu*

Plain flour   H/U: *Maida*   G: *Maido*   T: *Maida mavu*

Wheat provides the world with about 70 per cent of its calorie intake in the form of staple food. Wholemeal flour (*atta*) is obtained by grinding the grain in a flour mill or in a stone grinder (*chakki*). It is rich in bran, germ and vitamins. In India several forms of bread are prepared with wholemeal flour. Plain flour (*maida*) is obtained by sieving the bran and germ from the wholemeal. Three other popular products from wheat are semolina (*sooji* or *rava*), vermicelli (*sevian* or *sev*) and bulgar, and these are used for both savoury and sweet dishes.

PULSES

Pulses like bengal gram, black gram, cow gram, green gram, red lentil, red gram, and so on, are widely consumed. Pulses are indeed a good and cheap source of energy, protein, minerals and vitamins. They should be properly cooked before being eaten due to their high starch content. Germination of the pulses converts the starch into dextrose and maltose and these are more easily digestible. Pulses in either form are strongly recommended as a cheap source of nitrogen-rich protein food for vegetarians.

Bengal Gram or Chickpea
Whole   H/U: *Chana* or *kabuli chana*   G: *Chaniya*   T: *Kadalai*
Split   H/U: *Channa dhal*   G: *Chaniya dhal*   T: *Kothu kadalai*

There are several varieties but the two most popular are the small heart-shaped gram with a dark brown peel and the large, white, heart-shaped ones known as *kabuli chana*. Cook whole or split in spiced or plain form. Flour of the split gram *besan* or *channa atta* is used to prepare the famous Indian snack *bhajias* (see pages 83–6). When I was a young girl my *ayah* (maid) used to prepare a paste of *besan* and fresh cream and massage my face and body every week, saying it helped to lighten the complexion and soften the skin.

Black Gram
H/U: *Urad*   G: *Alad*   T: *Ulitham parrappu*

Black gram is used whole or split in various dishes but the most popular are the famous south Indian *idlis* (steamed cakes), *dosai* (fermented pancakes) and of course the *papadums*.

Cow Gram or Black-eyed Beans
H/U: *Lobia*   G: *Chora*   T: *Maramani*

The grains are greyish white in colour and shaped like a kidney and each one has a distinctive black eye. The other variety is the red kidney bean (*rajmah*). Both are very popular in the northern states of India and are cooked whole in various ways.

Green Gram
Whole   H/U: *Mung*   G: *Mug*   T: *Pachipayar*

Split   H/U: *Mung dhal*   G: *Mug ni dhal*
T: *Payathum parrappu*

Green gram is very rich in vitamins, iron and protein. Since bygone days it has been used in various religious ceremonies. *Koshumbri*, a salad made from germinated green gram (page 253), is one of the most delicious Indian side dishes. The water in which the pulse is soaked should not be thrown away but used in place of natural water as it is very cooling. Green gram flour is a very good substitute for soap – it does not remove your natural skin oil, only the dirt.

Red Lentil
Whole   H/U: *Masoor*   G/T: *Masur*

Peeled and split   H/U: *Masoor ki dhal*   G: *Masur ni dhal*
T: *Masur parrappu*

Whole or split red lentils are used in savoury dishes. Split red lentils are often cooked with rice to aid digestion and it is an Indian tradition to prepare *kitchdi* when there is someone sick in the house.

Red Gram or Pigeon Pea
H/U: *Arhar* or *tuvar*   G: *Tuvar ni dhal*   T: *Tuvaram parrappu*

Only split red grams are used. In the UK it is possible to buy them either dry or in a processed form which is lightly greased. It is the most commonly used pulse all over India, particularly in the south. Various curries of red gram blended with fresh vegetables or on its own are prepared and the most famous south Indian *rasam* (spiced broth – page 202).

SPICES AND HERBS

Indians are crowned as pioneers in the knowledge of spices and have been suppliers of these valuable food-processing agents for over 3500 years. Traders, warriors and explorers from various parts of the world brought their valuable merchandise, in the form of gold, silver and textiles, and exchanged them for Indian spices. Malabar on the west coast of India has been known as the 'spice kingdom'. Each spice not only provides its own flavouring but also its own medicinal value. There have been many folklore stories about herbs but it is a fact that they have medicinal values as well as flavour.

Asafoetida
H/U/G: *Hing*   T: *Perungayam*

Hing is obtained from the fresh roots of a perennial plant. It is dried and sold in block or powder form. It has an acrid and bitter taste and emits a strong odour. In bygone days it was tied in a bag and left hanging in one corner of the house. The smell was believed to be responsible for preventing diseases. It is now used as a flavouring agent in curries and pickles and is a very good digestive if used sparingly. Stores indefinitely in airtight jars.

Cardamom
H/U: *Elaichi*   G: *Elaychi*   T: *Elakkai*

Cardamom is called the 'queen of spices' and India exports about 90 per cent of cardamoms to the other countries in the world. There are two varieties. Green cardamom is used in both savoury and sweet dishes. The seeds are chewed to prevent bad breath and added to the famous *betel* leaf which is chewed by millions in India. It is also used to flavour tea and coffee (see page 271). Black cardamom is more aromatic and larger in size but only used in cooking. Both varieties store indefinitely in airtight jars. Powdered green cardamom seeds are also available but only from Indian grocers.

Chilli
H/U: *Mirchi*   G: *March*   T: *Milagai*

Chilli has become indispensable in the Indian cuisine for its extremely pungent and titillating taste. However, the chilli is no native of India. It was introduced to India by a group of adventurous sailors from Portugal who came across it in the regions of Peru. Therefore, no mention of it has been made in the ancient Indian Sanskritik literatures. Today, chilli is widely used in India although it is excluded from some dishes, especially from ceremonious food which is offered to the departed. Chillies are rich in vitamins A and C, and when dried and powdered they make cayenne pepper. In rural areas in India equal quantities of fresh green and red chillies are ground to a paste and eaten as an accompaniment to plain boiled rice. The bigger the chilli the less pungent it is. There are several kinds of chillies now available on the market. Some of the common varieties are country chilli, *sattur*, needle chilli, pot chilli, Kashmiri chilli and bird's eye chilli which is the most fiery. Some of them, like the Kashmiri chilli, only add colour to food and are not spicy at all. Fresh chillies can be frozen without blanching. Dried chillies and chilli powder store indefinitely in airtight jars. Commercially packaged chilli powders vary in strength and you may need to adjust the quantities.

Cinnamon
H/U: *Dalchini*   G: *Taj*   T: *Lavangapattai*

The best variety is a native of Ceylon. The shoots of a two-year-old cinnamon tree are cut and the bark is peeled after the branches have been exposed to air for about twenty-four hours. Then the bark is packed inside one another and dried. Cinnamon is found in long, brown cylindrical bark which is thin and brittle. It gives a sweetish, tingling, warm feeling when chewed, and is used in both savoury and sweet dishes. Stores indefinitely in airtight jars. When used in my recipes the length of the quill not the thickness is given. Available in powder form which also stores indefinitely.

Clove
H/U: *Lavang*   G: *Lavangi*   T: *Kirambu*

Clove trees belong to the family of *Eugenia jambulam* and are evergreen. The taste of the clove is pungent and tingling. In India cloves are used as spices and chewed with *betel* leaf from ancient times. When I was a young girl I was prone to fevers, and I remember my mother soaking a few cloves in water, rubbing them to obtain a paste and applying this to my temples. It was well-known in folklore medicine that this draws out the fever and also cools the patient. Cloves are used in both savoury and sweet culinary dishes and to spice tea and coffee (see page 271). They can be stored indefinitely in airtight jars and are also available in powder form.

31

Coriander Leaves

H/U: *Kothmir* or *bara dhaniya*   G: *Dhana*   T: *Kothamalli*

Coriander plants are extensively cultivated all over India for their aromatic leaves and seeds (see below). Fresh leaves are a must in every kind of curry to give an aromatic flavour. Fresh coriander can easily be grown from seeds and can be bought in bunches from Indian, Chinese and Greek grocers. It will stay fairly fresh for up to a week in the refrigerator, or can be frozen by two methods. A simple method is to break the leaves and the very tender stems and open freeze. When frozen, pack in polythene bags or airtight boxes. To use, just crush a little with your fingers while still frozen and return the rest to the freezer. Alternatively, you can grind the leaves and stems in oil in an electric blender and freeze in icetrays. When the cubes are set, store in polythene bags.

Coriander

H/U: *Dhaniya*   G: *Dhana*   T: *Kothamalli virai*

Coriander seeds are dried when they ripen. They are brownish yellow in colour and measure about 5mm in diameter. On each half of the seed there are five wavy ridges. They have an aromatic odour and an agreeable spicy taste. Seeds can be stored indefinitely but I recommend that you make small quantities when powdering to retain its freshness and aroma. The powder of roasted coriander seeds is blended with other spices to prepare curry powder. When grinding to a powder it is advisable to dry-roast the seeds first (see page 48). Coriander powder adds flavour to and thickens curries.

Cumin

H/U: *Zeera*   G: *Jeera*   T: *Jeerakam*

Cumin is a brown seed about 4–6mm long, an elongated oval shape tapering at both ends. Cumin resembles caraway seeds but they should not be mistaken for one another as they are totally different in flavour. Cumin seeds are largely used in condiments, perfumery and cosmetics. The seeds are sweet and aromatic. Seeds can be stored indefinitely in airtight jars but powder should be prepared in small batches following the same method as for coriander seeds (see page 32).

Curry Leaves
H/U: *Kariyapath*　　G: *Mitho limdo*　　T: *Karvepillai*

The curry leaf tree grows in the damp and hot parts of India. Curry leaves have an aromatic flavour and are used along with other spices to flavour curries. If you are planning to buy a packet, here are two hints for storage. Place the leaves open in a wicker basket in a dry place. Gradually they will become dull brown and brittle. Do not cover or seal the dried leaves or they will become mouldy. Alternatively, open freeze the leaves and when frozen seal in an airtight container. The leaves remain separate so you can easily remove only the number required.

When I was on my teaching course a student brought in a herb called 'curry herb' which she had bought from a garden centre. This only has a faint curry aroma and will not provide the same flavouring as authentic curry leaves.

Fennel
H/U: *Saunf*　　G: *Varialli*　　T: *Peerumjeerakam*

Fennel seeds are greenish yellow or yellowish brown and oblong in shape. They are aromatic and have a sweet and agreeable taste. Chewing some dry roasted seeds every day after meals prevents bad breath and indigestion. Whole seeds can be stored indefinitely but only prepare small batches of powder to retain the freshness and delightful aroma.

Garlic
H/U: *Lehsan*　　G: *Lasan*　　T: *Ullipundu*

Garlic is the common flavouring bulb of the plant *allium sativum* and is considered to be the 'queen of herbs'. In India garlic has been commonly used for centuries in vegetarian and non-vegetarian curries, various chutneys and pickles, and as a medicine to cure various diseases. The taste of garlic is an irritant to some and it emits a strong pungent smell. Garlic also has an antibacterial effect and checks the cholesterol in the body. Its regular use in the preservation of food and health is part of our cultural heritage. Garlic produces warmth in the body during the winter months and causes profuse perspiration during the summer months which keeps one fresh and cool. Every November at home in India, my mother serves garlic tops with eggs (page 144) with *mung dhal kitchdi*. This is her answer to central heating and she says it will provide us with 'heat' for the winter months. Here you can serve this in May or June when the tops of the garlic growing in the garden (or in a pot) are young and green. Fresh garlic cloves can be peeled, frozen open, and then sealed in polythene bags, or ground with oil to a paste and stored in the freezer in small portions (see page 56).

Ginger
H/U: *Adrak*   G: *Adu*   T: *Inji*

Ginger is a perennial, horizontal and knotty root. It is fibrous and has a pungent aromatic taste. Ginger is cultivated all over India but the ginger grown in the state of Kerala is superior in aroma and taste. Fresh ginger is usually used to enhance the appetite. Chewing a piece of fresh ginger after meals is an insurance against indigestion. If you do not like the taste of fresh ginger, make up some ginger conserve (*adrak ka murraba* – page 249). Peeled fresh ginger can be stored by following the same method as for garlic (page 33). For ground method, see page 56.

Mace and Nutmeg
H/U: *Javithri* or *jaiphal*   G: *Jaypathri* or *jaifal*
T: *Jathipatri* or *jattikkai*

Mace and nutmeg are the products of the same tree,

myrustuca fragrans. Mace is the dried, thin covering of the fruit and the dried kernel is the nutmeg. Mace is mainly used in savoury dishes but nutmeg is used in both savoury and sweet. Both can be stored indefinitely in airtight jars.

Mint
H/U: *Phudina*   G: *Pudina*   T: *Pothina*

Mint is a very aromatic herb which is common all over India. However, Indian mint is very different to the mint available in the UK. In olden days it is believed that Mentha, the damsel lover of the god Pluto, was transformed into this herb due to the anger of Prosarpain, wife of Pluto and goddess of wealth. Mint is therefore known as *mentha* in Latin. Mint leaves can be stored in the freezer by the same method as for coriander leaves (page 32).

Omum
H/U: *Ajwain*   G: *Ajma*   T: *Omum*

The *ujwain* plant belongs to the coriander family but resembles the dill plant and grows to a metre high. The dry seeds are harvested and are ovate, about 2mm long and 1mm broad. They taste aromatic, sharp, tingling and slightly bitter. Popularly used by Gujeratis and added to pickles. Stores indefinitely.

Onion Seeds
H/U/G: *Kalonji*

This spice is a small, black, teardrop-shaped seed, with a delicious earthy aroma and taste, and is used mainly by north Indians in vegetable dishes or sprinkled on unleavened bread. Stores indefinitely.

Sinapis or Mustard Seeds
H/U/G: *Rai*   T: *Kadagu*

Black mustard is an annual herbaceous plant largely cultivated in tropical countries. The dry seeds are small, round and darkish brown or greyish brown in colour, and about 1mm in diameter. Seeds are odourless but when they are pounded and moistened with water they have a pungent odour. Mustard is internationally used as an appetizer, flavouring agent and food preservative. Its presence in food and pickles prevents the growth of black fungus. In India mustard seeds are fried in oil with cumin seeds and curry leaves to temper vegetable and lentil dishes in their final cooking stage (see page 49). Can be stored indefinitely. When the seeds are planted they produce *sarson kar sag*, a very popular green leafy vegetable in India.

Tamarind
H/U: *Imli*   G: *Amli*   T: *Pulli*

The tamarind tree is a native of south India. It is an ornamental tree with a life span of 120 years. The leaves and the pinkish white flowers are sour in taste. The crescent-shaped fruit is a legume measuring 5–15cm long. When tender the fruit is a green epicarp with a soft brown peel. As the fruit ripens the covering becomes hard and brittle and the pulp becomes dark maroon, with strings of fibres and about seven to ten large brown seeds. When the outer covering is fully dry the fruits are plucked and the pulp separated from the fibres and seeds to be sold in packets. This can easily be mistaken for preserved dates, so check carefully. Tamarind is extensively used in curries all over India as the pulp has a sour-sweet taste. It is available in a purified concentrated form in jars and also in diluted juice form. All varieties can be obtained from India and Chinese shops and can be stored indefinitely. Several recipes call for tamarind juice: see page 60 for method.

Turmeric
H/U: *Haldi*   G: *Haldar*   T: *Manjal*

Turmeric is obtained from the roots of a perennial plant. It is sold in dried pieces or powdered form. The taste and smell of turmeric are aromatic and pungent. It is largely used in India as a flavouring and colouring agent in curries and condiments, for dyeing material, and, above all, it is considered a very sacred article in all religious and social ceremonies in India. A teaspoon of turmeric powder with cream, sandal powder and bengal gram flour applied once daily is an excellent cosmetic to keep the face flower-fresh and velvet-smooth. In India most brides are bathed after their body has been massaged with this paste the day before, or very early in the morning on the day of, their wedding. Can be stored indefinitely in airtight jars.

Zaffran/Saffron

H/U: *Zaffran*   G: *Zafran* or *kesari*   T: *Kesar*

The world's most expensive spice. This is understandable when you realize that it requires nearly 100,000 crocus blossoms, picked by hand, to produce a pound of saffron. The saffron comes from the stigmas, which are also removed by hand. Each crocus has only three stigmas. Once native only to southern Europe and Asia, the saffron crocus is now widely cultivated in Mexico and California. To use, soak a few strands in a little warm milk or water. Powdered saffron can be used for colouring, but use only authentic saffron strands when it is the flavour that is required. In India it is used in curries and rice dishes, but mostly in sweet dishes. Never use turmeric as a substitute, either for flavouring or colouring. Can be stored indefinitely in airtight jars.

NUTS AND SEEDS

The various types of nuts that we eat every day are highly nutritious. They are packed with concentrated food components and are therefore required in lesser quantities. There are several varieties but those popularly used in India are almond, cudapah almond, peanut, walnut, cashew nut, coconut and pistachio nut.

Almond
H/U/G/T: *Badam*

100g (4 oz) of shelled almonds will supply as much vitamin B_1 and protein as one gets by eating any of the following foods: 400g (14 oz) beef or 250g (9 oz) mutton or 6 eggs or 2½ cups milk. In India almonds are used whole, flaked, or coarsely or finely ground.

Cashew Nut
H/U: *Kaju*   G: *Kazu*   T: *Mundiriparrappu*

Roasted cashew nuts are very nutritious and fattening. Cashew nuts are mainly used as a snack in Western countries but in India they are used in both savoury and sweet dishes.

Coconut
H/U: *Nariyal*   G: *Narial*   T: *Thenga*

The Hindu holy scriptures named the coconut tree the Tree of Heavens. To the south Indian in particular the coconut tree is very sacred and they are tended like children. The coconut tree provides all the bare necessities. The refreshing water is used to quench thirst, the ripe kernel is used as food, the sap provides sugar, the shells are made into utensils, the dried leaves are used for roofing, and from the fibrous tissues in the stem we make clothes, mats, sails for ships and rope for towing. Finally, the oil is used for cooking, conditioning hair and lighting lamps. With all these uses the coconut tree is aptly called the Tree of Heavens. A number of recipes require coconut milk: see pages 58–60 for methods of extracting coconut milk. Study them carefully and then decide on the one that will suit you best.

Peanut or Groundnut
H/U: *Phalli*   G: *Bhoising* or *mandvi*   T: *Nilakkadala*

There are a number of varieties but in India the pods with two seeds are very common. It is said that Mahatma Gandhi, the father of the Indian nation, used to eat groundnuts with goat's milk every day. People living to a ripe age believe that the secret of their longevity lies in eating groundnuts.

Pistachio Nut
H/U: *Pista*   G: *Pishta*   T: *Pista parrappu*

Pistachio nuts are imported from Iran, Syria and Afghanistan. They are covered with a brown paper-like skin and the kernel is yellowish green. Sweet and nutritious, these nuts are mainly used in sweet dishes or garnish.

Walnut
H/U/G: *Akhrot*   T: *Nattu akrotu kottai*

Walnuts are also imported into India from Iran and Afghanistan. They are used in sweetmeats, salads, *raitha* (walnuts mixed with yogurt) or as a garnish. Eating a few walnuts after fatty foods prevents indigestion.

Poppy Seeds
H/U: *Khuskhus*   G: *Kuskus*   T: *Kasakasa*

Poppy seeds are used in many curries where the gravy needs to be thick because in India it is taboo to thicken any curry with flour or other starches. Poppy seeds are also sprinkled on several Indian breads. Many recipes call for ground poppy seeds. As they are very difficult to grind finely, I recommend you to dry-roast them a little longer than the other ingredients and grind them first on their own before adding the other ingredients. This will give the poppy seeds more chance to break up. They can be stored indefinitely in airtight jars.

Sesame or Gingelly Seeds
H/U: *Til*   G: *Tul*   T: *Ellu*

Sesame seeds have a nutty flavour and are used in curries which need thickening. Also used on breads and the famous *til-ki-chikki* (sesame and jaggery biscuits). In India sesame oil (*til-ka-tel*), which has a different flavour to the refined Chinese variety, is popularly used in cooking. Seeds and oil can be stored indefinitely.

FRUITS

Fruits have been eaten by mankind from time immemorial; in fact Adam, 'the first man', ate the 'forbidden apple'. The Vedas (Hindu holy scriptures) state that fruits form the basis of the foods of gods. It is believed that when Lord Shiva saw that the heavenly mango fruit, the favourite fruit of his consort Parvathi, did not exist on earth he created mango trees on this beautiful part of the earth to please her. The Holy Quran states that fruit like grapes, dates, figs, olives and pomegranates are heavenly gifts from the gods. All this suggests that fruit is health-giving and health-promoting. The following are some of the fruits popularly cultivated in India.

Apple (*sep*), apricot (*khubani*), banana (*kela*), bullock's heart (*ramphal*), chikkoo (*sapota*), custard apple (*sitaphal*), dates (*khajur*), figs (*anjeer*), grapes (*angoor*), guava (*amrud*), jackfruit (*phanuss*), lime (*nimbu*), loquat (*lokat*), mango (*aamb*), muskmelon (*kharbuz*), orange (*santra*), papaya (*papita*), passion fruit (*passion phal*), peach (*arhu*), pear (*perus*), pineapple (*ananas*), plum (*alucha*), pomegranate (*anar*), pomelo (*chakotra*), sweet lime (*mosambi*), tomato or love apple (*tamatar*), toddy fruit (*sendola*), watermelon (*tarbuz*), wood apple (*kayth*) and zyzyphus (*bair*).

With the exception of sweet lime, toddy fruit and wood apple, I have been able to buy all these fruits from large Indian and Chinese grocers and a number of them are also stocked by supermarkets and large food halls.

Banana
H/U/G: *Kela*   T: *Vazhaikai*

Banana plants are cultivated in abundance all over India. The banana plant and fruit are considered to be auspicious in all religious and social ceremonies in India. Banana is a food-fruit for the masses, and there are many varieties in India. Plaintain (*kacha kela*), raw banana, ordinary long bananas, dwarf bananas, red bananas and *ras-bale*. Red banana, *ras-bale* and raw bananas are used in curries or made into delicious fritters. The entire plant is used in India: the stems are used as fodder, the flowers for cooking, the fruits for eating and the leaves are used as plates, which bear cleanliness and are said to increase the appetite. Foodstuffs are also wrapped in them to be steamed. They have one further use, as decoration around the *mandap* (wedding altar) and around the gates through which the wedding guests are welcomed.

Guava
H/U: *Amrud*   G: *Jamruk*   T: *Koyya pazam*

Guava is extensively grown all over India and there are more than a dozen varieties. The guava tree is evergreen and most homes have one. As it is extremely rich in vitamin C, this fruit should be eaten regularly, either raw or made into ice cream, cakes or jelly.

Lime
H/U: *Limbu*   G: *Nimbu*   T: *Elumichhai pazam*

Some people think that a lime and a lemon are the same, but this is not so. The lime is smaller and round, its peel is thin and sweetish and it contains less juice. Unlike lemons, limes are suitable for pickling. In India lime also plays a prominent role in cosmetics. When I was a young girl my mother dried lime peels and then powdered them. This was then mixed with glycerine and I used it to massage my face.

Mango
H/U: *Aamb*   G: *Keri*   T: *Mama pazam*

Mango is one of the oldest fruits cultivated in India from

ancient times, perhaps for as long as 4000–6000 years. There are several varieties but the most popular are *alfonso* (available in season – April/May – in the UK), *langra, malgoba, neelam, raspuri, shahpasand* and *totapuri*. The pleasure of eating this fruit has earned it the title of 'king of fruits'. Ripe mangoes are eaten raw, made into desserts, ice cream, cakes, jelly, preserves and squash. Green or unripe mangoes are used in curries or made into a hundred different varieties of pickles and chutneys. One could write a complete book on Indian mango pickles as each community has its own variation, but the recipe on page 247 would be considered 'general' throughout India. When making mango pickle in India there are some rules to abide by. Hands, vessels and jars should be sterilized. It is never prepared or served after the sun sets. A housewife never prepares or even handles it during menstruation. It has also been said that mango pickle will go mouldy if prepared by someone who is unhappy or surrounded by unhappiness.

In season mango trees attract monkeys but the Hindus never shoo them away as they worship Hanuman – the 'monkey god' who helped Rama save his beloved Sita who had been abducted to Sri Lanka by the demon Raavana.

Papaya/Pawpaw
H/U: *Papita* or *papaya*   G: *Papanvu*   T: *Papali pazam*

Papaya is a native of South America and has been cultivated in India since the Portuguese sailors introduced it in the eighteenth century. It is interesting to note that when papaya was introduced to Europe, women were the first to use it as a cosmetic. One writer affirms that Josephine, the Empress of France, applied the pulp of papaya as a cleansing cream on her face, neck and arms. Some women thought that this fruit possessed the remarkable quality of removing unwanted flesh from any part of the body. Marco Polo left behind a record in India which showed that papaya was used by the sailors of his time to cure scurvy and dysentery. Ripe papaya is eaten raw, made into desserts, ice cream, drinks and jelly. Raw papaya is used like a vegetable and in India the paste is used as a meat tenderizer.

Tomato or Love Apple
H/U: *Tamatar*   G: *Tamota*   T: *Thakkali pazam*

Tomatoes, like a few other fruits and vegetables, were introduced to India by the Portuguese in the eighteenth century. At first orthodox families were against the use of any new fruits and vegetables. It was easy for the elders to get away with this by referring to new fruits and vegetables as forbidden by religious leaders. However, tomatoes soon became established and today rich and poor homes alike cannot do without them. In India they are used to make curries and chutneys, salads, sauces, drinks and sorbet, and as a garnish.

DAIRY PRODUCTS

Milk
H/U/G: *Doodh*   T: *Pallu*

A Harvard University professor said that 'Milk is the only single article of food that fairly represents a complete diet. It has no equal for the promotion of growth as nutrition.' Milk forms the main base of hundreds of delicious Indian sweets and is placed among the high-ranking religious foods. In India when we move into a new house or welcome a new bride we let a pan of milk boil over, thus spreading prosperity. Hot milk with honey and a pinch of turmeric is very soothing for an irritating cough.

Cream
H/U: *Balai*   G: *Malai*   T: *Paaladai*

The fat that appears on the surface of warmed milk can be collected in the form of cream. Indian cream is different in texture to the cream available in the West. My favourite breakfast used to be thick fresh cream with jam eaten with hot chappatis. Cream is delicious but one's daily intake should not exceed 50g (2 oz). Application of cream over the face an hour before you go to bed is a very good moisturizer.

Butter
H/U: *Maska* or *makhan*   G: *Makkan*   T: *Vennai*

Butter is made by churning the cream. During this process all the fat runs into a solid mass and forms butter. Commercial butter was only just making its way into the shops when I left India in 1965. Until then every family churned their own. Eating bread and butter for breakfast is considered fashionable and therefore this custom is mainly followed by the rich and middle classes. Like cream, you should control your intake of butter.

Clarified Butter/Ghee
H/U/G: *Ghee*   T: *Neyi*

Ghee is made by melting butter in water until the water has evaporated. It is a most popular cooking fat which is flavoursome and nutritious. Eggs fried in ghee is a popular breakfast dish. Ghee is also spread over freshly baked chappatis and *parathas* and is always sprinkled over hot rice to purify the rice before it is consumed – an act which has been practised since ancient times. It is used at every religious ceremony and marriages, and *prasadams* (any cooked item offered to presiding deities in famous temples and then to pilgrims free of charge) are only cooked in ghee. If you have access to an Indian grocer, purchase a good quality ghee and try it. Alternatively, use unsalted butter or a good quality vegetable oil.

Yogurt
H/U: *Dahi*   G: *Dhai*   T: *Tayir*

Yogurt is prepared by the action of a special kind of

'starter' having a different kind of lactic acid bacillus called *lactobacillus bulgaricus*. A simple method is as follows:

> ½ litre (1 pint) milk
> 1 tablespoon natural yogurt (starter)

Bring the milk to the boil in a large saucepan. When it rises remove from the heat. Allow the milk to cool to the point when you can dip your finger in it without flinching or to baby's feed temperature. Beat the yogurt in a cup and mix in a little warm milk. When smooth pour into a glass or earthen dish and add the rest of the warm milk and mix well. Cover the dish and place in a warm area to set. Depending on the warmth around the dish the yogurt will set in 6–8 hours. (I place it on my central heating boiler and the yogurt sets in 3–4 hours.) During the summer months I leave it in the oven or airing cupboard. Alternatively, you can prepare it in a wide mouth vacuum flask.

Buttermilk
H/U/G: *Lassi* or *chans*   T: *Mor*

Buttermilk is prepared by churning yogurt and adding some water, and then removing the fat in the form of butter. This process is common all over India. Fatty buttermilk can also be prepared by churning yogurt with extra water and leaving the fat. The butter from this process is a favourite of the Sikhs and Punjabis in India. Buttermilk is a refreshing drink, either sweet or savoury.

Cheese
H/U/G: *Paneer*

Like butter, it is only in recent years that processed cheese has been sold in shops in India. Until then families made their own cheese and this was done by adding rennet, or a souring agent like lime juice, to boiling milk to make it curdle. This is then wrapped in muslin and put under pressure for 2–3 hours to remove all the whey. The cheese collected in the muslin is then ready to eat. It is very popular in vegetarian dishes, adding body and bite. The quality and yield of *paneer* depends entirely on the richness of the milk. In India *paneer* is only made from cow's milk. I learned the art of making *paneer* last year under the guidance of my mother who was visiting me from India. This is how I prepare it.

> 1.2 litres (2 pints) milk
> fresh lime or lemon juice or bottled lemon juice
>   (1 tablespoon to every 2½ cups of milk)
> a large clean piece muslin for straining
> 2 tablespoons full cream milk powder
> 1 tablespoon plain flour

Bring milk to the boil stirring slowly all the time to avoid any cream forming on the surface. When the milk has boiled remove from the heat and add the lemon juice. This will make the milk curdle. Allow to rest till the curdled milk has settled at the bottom and the whey has risen to the surface. Without disturbing the curdled milk, gently pour off as much of the whey as possible collecting it for further use (see below). Place the muslin over a large bowl or in a large sieve. Put the curdled milk on the muslin cloth and tie the corners. Allow it to hang until all the whey has drained. Knead the *paneer* until smooth, adding milk powder and flour. Flatten it out and return it to the muslin. Wrap the muslin over and place a heavy object on it. I usually use a plate with a heavy object on top. Allow it to rest under the weight for about 30 minutes as this will remove any excess whey.

WHEY   The whey should not be thrown away as it is a very nutritious liquid-food for invalids and a good thirst-quencher. Drink it hot with salt and pepper and a few drops of lemon juice, or cold with a pinch of salt and honey.

Eggs

H/U: *Anda*   G: *Indu* or *baida*   T: *Muttai*

In India a great percentage of people cannot afford eggs but try to make sure you and your family eat one egg at least once in two days. Eggs store well in a cool place without refrigeration. In India when we buy eggs we put them in water. If they sink they are fresh but if they float they are not. Aim for the non-shiny shells and when you crack an egg the yolk should be firm and round.

Basic Preparations and Cooking Methods

UTENSILS AND EQUIPMENT

Just three which deserve a mention.

For deep-frying in India we use a *karai*. This is very similar to a wok, made of thin metal, and available in many sizes. You can use a traditional wok or a non-stick wok, but if you do not want to invest in either of these, use a deep, heavy frying pan. Do remember that foods fried in under-heated oil or ghee become greasy. To prevent this, heat the oil or ghee to smoking point before starting to fry.

Many Indian breads and pancakes are roasted and for this we use a *tava*. This is a heavy metal griddle and a good quality one lasts a lifetime. Its regular use gets it fully seasoned and the older a *tava* the better. You can use a scot girdle or a cast-iron frying pan.

An electric blender is a vital piece of equipment as so many recipes call for ingredients to be ground. In India the old-fashioned method is still preferred. A heavy oblong stone with a heavy stone rolling pin is used and if they were not so heavy I would have carried one back from India. The ingredients are placed on the washed oblong stone and ground backwards and forwards with the rolling pin, adding water or oil. See notes below on how to grind ingredients in an electric blender.

WEIGHTS AND MEASURES

Throughout the book both metric and imperial weights have been given. Use only one set of weights and measures as they are not interchangeable. For measuring rice and water I have used cup measures. Use the same cup to measure both the rice and the water.

Cup and spoon measures are level.

HOW TO GRIND OR POUND SPICES AND HERBS

In many of the recipes which follow you will notice that I list separately the ingredients that have to be ground or pounded. This can be done in an electric blender. If the amount to be ground or pounded is very small you can use a small electric coffee grinder. When grinding in an electric blender add oil to facilitate the grinding. This acts as a lubricant and will prolong the life of the blender (water and other liquids tend to rust the motor). If you have used oil for grinding, the ground paste can be fried without oil.

Dry-roasting Method

When whole spices need to be ground I recommend that they are dry-roasted first. Heat a griddle or a heavy frying pan and fry each spice individually without oil until fragrant. Turn the spices regularly with a spatula to avoid burning. Roasting spices brings out the flavour as well as making grinding easier.

Some recipes need ground poppy seeds which are very difficult to grind to a smooth paste. Roast them well and grind them on their own first. Then add the remaining ingredients gradually. By doing this you will give the poppy seeds more of a chance to break up.

Some recipes require coconut to be browned and ground. Use desiccated coconut which can be browned on a griddle or in a frying pan. They brown very fast, so be careful – if you brown them too much it will give your dish a bitter taste and a very dark colour.

Final Fry (*Tarka* or *baghar*)

Several dishes call for a final fry, especially lentil dishes. You have to work very fast and be careful not to get the hot oil on yourself. Heat the oil until nearly smoking and fry the spices whole until they begin to splutter. Standing well back pour the oil and spices on to the vegetables or lentils and cover the pan immediately to retain the aroma. Mustard seeds are generally fried first and when they start to pop drop in the remaining ingredients.

Addition of spices while cooking Always reduce the heat before adding any powdered spices as they burn very easily and will give your dish a bitter taste. If you are worried about burning the spices use my method. I mix powdered spices, like coriander, cumin, turmeric and chilli powder, in a little water and fry them gently until the water has evaporated and the oil separated from the spices.

Cooking vegetables in their own juices Most vegetables have a certain amount of water in them and you can cook them in their own juices. Unless the recipe specifies a gravy of thin consistency, add the smallest amount of water necessary. By doing this you not only retain the nutritive quality of the vegetables but you do not overcook them. In order to prevent vegetables from charring as a result of water evaporating inside the utensil, you can cover the pan with a pyrex plate and pour some water on to the plate. If you are using a non-stick wok you can pour some water on the hollow of the lid where the knob is. If you need to add water in the middle of cooking, always add hot water as cold water will change the cooking temperature.

Hot curries I have used chilli powder in most of the recipes but the quantity used (unless the dish is meant to be hot) should be palatable by all. If by accident any dish has become too hot, temper it with some lime or lemon juice and a little sugar. Alternatively, serve natural yogurt as an accompaniment which will act as a 'fire extinguisher'. Drink plain water with your meal to cool your mouth as beer or other alcoholic drinks have sharp, sweet or bitter tastes and will only make your tongue tingle more. End your meal by eating a little plain rice or bread, as this will absorb some of the chilli taste.

Seasoning A recommended quantity of salt is given with each recipe but adjust this to suit your own taste. I tend to eat less salt so my suggestions should be used as a guide only. If your dish has accidentally become too salty adjust by adding a few drops of lime or lemon juice. If the dish has a lot of gravy you can add a piece of bread or *chappati* dough. The bread and dough will absorb some of the excess salt, but should be discarded before serving.

Stains Curry stains are lethal due to the strong dye in turmeric powder. Stained tablecloths or clothes need to be boil-washed, but if they are coloured this may not be possible. Immediately curry spills on any garment sprinkle it with talcum powder or some dry flour as this will absorb some of the stain. Stained cutlery and crockery can be cleaned by soaking them in hot water to which used tea leaves have been added; alternatively, rub them with some softened tamarind and leave them aside for a few minutes before rinsing.

Aftertaste After the meal you can try any of the following to freshen your mouth.
1. Chew a few lightly roasted fennel seeds.
2. Chew a few cardamom seeds.
3. Suck a slice of lime, lemon or orange, sprinkled with salt and pepper. This is not only refreshing but the acid in these fruits helps break up fat.
4. Drink chilled sweetened water with lime or lemon juice and rose essence.

Shopping. Most of the spices are now readily available. There are several Indian grocers dotted throughout the UK and most supermarkets and food halls offer a good range. To purchase by mail order, write to Viniron Ltd, 119 Drummond Street, London NW1 2HL (tel: 01-387 8653).

Powdered spice mixtures and pastes If you are an Indian-food fanatic try making up small batches of your own spice mixtures and pastes. I have given a few variations below. If you decide to use any one of these in a recipe then omit or add spices accordingly. I have suggested small quantities as it is important to retain their lovely aromas. Once you have either powdered them or ground them to a paste, store them in sterilized airtight jars, clearly labelled with the ingredients of each mixture for easy reference.

Simple Spice Mixture

90g (3½ oz) coriander seeds   *8g (¼ oz) turmeric powder*
15g (½ oz) cumin seeds
30g (1 oz) whole red chillies
  (seeded for milder flavour)

Individually dry-roast each spice, except the turmeric powder, until aromatic. Cool. Grind together to a fine powder in an electric blender or coffee grinder. (A word of warning: if your blender or grinder has a plastic bowl the turmeric dye will stain it. To avoid this grind the coriander seeds, cumin seeds and chillies and then add the turmeric powder and pass through a dry sieve. This way you will ensure even distribution of the spices.) Use 1 tablespoon of this powder for every 450g (1 lb) vegetables.

wder 1 Very Mild

90g (3½ oz) coriander seeds
30g (1 oz) whole red chillies
  (seed, or reduce quantity
  to suit your taste)
10 black peppercorns

2 5-cm (2-inch) quills
  cinnamon
4 cloves
1 tablespoon fennel seeds
8g (¼ oz) turmeric powder

To grind follow the same method as for the Simple Spice
Mixture (page 51).

Curry Powder 2 Mild

90g (3½ oz) coriander seeds
8g (¼ oz) large dry red
  chillies (kashmiri)
10 black peppercorns
1 5-cm (2-inch) quill
  cinnamon

2 cloves
1 teaspoon fennel seeds
1 tablespoon turmeric
  powder

To grind follow the same method as for Simple Spice Mixture
(page 51).

Curry Powder 3 Medium Hot

90g (3½ oz) coriander seeds
15g (½ oz) small whole dry
  chillies ('bird's eyes')
15g (½ oz) black
  peppercorns
8g (¼ oz) mustard seeds
15g (½ oz) cumin seeds
8g (¼ oz) sesame seeds

8g (¼ oz) poppy seeds
1 tablespoon split bengal
  gram (channa dhal)
4 cloves
2 5-cm (2-inch) quills
  cinnamon
4 peeled cardamoms
8g (¼ oz) turmeric powder

To grind follow the same method as for Simple Spice Mixture
(page 51). The poppy seeds need a good roasting to ensure
fine powdering (see page 48).

Curry Powder 4 Very Hot ✳

125g (5 oz) coriander seeds
125g (5 oz) whole red chillies
  (seed, or reduce quantity to
  suit your taste)
75g (2½ oz) split bengal
  gram (channa dhal)

¼ teaspoon fenugreek seeds
10 black peppercorns
15g (½ oz) turmeric powder
20 dried curry leaves

To grind follow the same method as for the Simple Spice Mixture (page 51).

Goda Masala
Maharashtran Spice Mixture

125g (5 oz) coriander seeds
25g (1 oz) cumin seeds
25g (1 oz) dry coconut
  (copra)
25g (1 oz) sesame seeds
6 cloves
2 5-cm (2-inch) quills
  cinnamon

¼ teaspoon fenugreek seeds
1 teaspoon split black gram
  (urad dhal)
8g (¼ oz) whole dry red
  chillies
15g (½ oz) turmeric powder
¼ teaspoon asafoetida
10 dry curry leaves

To grind follow the same method as for Simple Spice Mixture (page 51).

Sambhar Powder 1
Spice Mixture for Lentils

25g (1 oz) coriander seeds
8g (¼ oz) whole dry red
  chillies
1 teaspoon split black gram
  (urad dhal)

½ teaspoon fenugreek seeds
1 teaspoon mustard seeds
½ teaspoon turmeric powder
¼ teaspoon asafoetida

To grind follow the same method as for Simple Spice Mixture (page 51). Two heaped tablespoons of this powder may be used for 8 cups *sambhar* – thick lentil curry.

Sambhar Powder 2

75g (3 oz) coriander seeds	*1 teaspoon mustard seeds*
15g (½ oz) split bengal gram	*½ teaspoon asafoetida*
(channa dhal)	*20g (2 oz) dry coconut*
8g (¼ oz) split black gram	(copra)
(urad dhal)	*50g (2 oz) sesame seeds*
8g (¼ oz) black peppercorns	*1 tablespoon turmeric*
¼ teaspoon fenugreek seeds	*powder*
50g (2 oz) whole dried red	*20 dry curry leaves*
chillies	

To grind follow the same method as for Simple Spice Mixture (page 51).

Sambhar Powder 3

Use same ingredients as Sambhar Powder 2 but delete sesame seeds and add 25g (1 oz) split red gram (*arbar* or *tuvar*).

Rasam Masala
Spiced Broth Mixture

75g (3 oz) coriander seeds	*2 tablespoons cumin seeds*
25g (1 oz) whole black	*1 tablespoon mustard seeds*
peppercorns	*1 tablespoon split bengal*
15g (½ oz) whole dry red	*gram* (channa dhal)
chillies	*2 teaspoons turmeric powder*

To grind follow the same method as for Simple Spice Mixture (page 51).

Garam Masala

Garam masala is a fragrant mixture of spices like cardamoms, cloves, cinnamon, nutmeg, and so on, added to dishes in the final stages of cooking or sprinkled over the top just before serving. I have specified the quantity to be used, but which particular garam masala you use I leave up to you. There are five variations. Or you can use a ready-made garam masala which can be bought from Indian and Chinese grocers and supermarkets.

Garam Masala 1
Fragrant Spice Mixture

25g (1 oz) peeled cardamom seeds
40g (1½ oz) cloves
40g (1½ oz) cinnamon
40g (1½ oz) black peppercorns

To grind follow the same method as for Simple Spice Mixture (page 51).

Garam Masala 2

3 tablespoons cumin seeds
6 tablespoons coriander seeds
40g (1½ oz) cloves
25g (1 oz) peeled cardamom seeds
40g (1½ oz) cinnamon
40g (1½ oz) black peppercorns

To grind follow the same method as for Simple Spice Mixture (page 51).

Garam Masala 3

Use same ingredients as garam masala 2 but add 1 whole grated nutmeg. (Nutmeg need not be dry-roasted.)

Garam Masala 4
Kashmiri Style

Use same ingredients as garam masala 2 but delete cumin seeds and coriander seeds and add 2 tablespoons black cumin seeds (*shahjeera*) and half a grated nutmeg.

Garam Masala 5

Use same ingredients as for garam masala 1 but delete peppercorns and add 1 tablespoon of mace.

Basic Ginger or Garlic Paste

Ginger and garlic are used in most recipes and I find pastes prepared in advance save a lot of time and wastage. Adjust the quantity that you make according to the amount you will use. I prepare 2.5kg (5 lb) of each and this sees me through the whole year.

Ginger Paste
2.5 kg (5 lb) fresh ginger   *approximately 2½ cups oil*
5 tablespoons salt   *for grinding and storing*

Wash, peel and coarsely cut the ginger. Grind the ginger with salt in an electric blender, using oil to facilitate the grinder. Store in small airtight containers in the freezer, or freeze in ice-cube trays. When the cubes are set store in plastic bags. One cube is approximately 2 teaspoons when thawed.

Garlic Paste
2.5kg (5 lb) garlic   *approximately 2½ cups oil*
5 tablespoons salt   *for grinding and storing*

Break the garlic pods into cloves and leave them in a tray or a wicker basket for about 24 hours in a dry warm place. This will make the peel a little brittle and easier to remove. To grind follow the same method as for ginger paste (above). To store follow the same method as for ginger paste. One cube is approximately 2 teaspoons when thawed.

Hara Masala
Green Spice Paste

It is very handy to have this paste in your larder as its addition to any dish enhances the flavour. A similar paste is also available from Indian grocers.

12 cloves garlic, peeled	*1 teaspoon fenugreek seeds,*
4 2.5-cm (1-inch) pieces	*soaked overnight to swell*
ginger, peeled	*2 teaspoons salt*
1 cup tightly packed mint	*2 teaspoons turmeric powder*
leaves	*1 teaspoon ground cloves*
1 cup tightly packed coriander	*1 teaspoon ground cinnamon*
leaves and tender stems	*³/4 cup oil*
¹/2 cup vinegar	

Put the garlic, ginger, mint leaves and coriander leaves and stems in an electric blender. Blend on a high speed for a few minutes, adding vinegar to facilitate the blender. Add the fenugreek seeds and blend until you have a smooth paste. Add the salt and powdered spices and blend for a further 1 minute to ensure even distribution. Heat the oil in a large heavy pan or a wok and when it nearly reaches smoking point add the blended mixture and bring to the boil, stirring occasionally. Remove from heat and allow the mixture to cool completely before storing in airtight jars.

This mixture has a long larder life if there is always some oil floating above the mixture. Once you have started using the mixture (always use a clean dry spoon) and find that the oil level has dropped, heat a little more oil, cool it and add to the jar.

Lal Masala
Red Spice Paste

Another useful paste for your larder, especially if you have forgotten to buy ginger and garlic. A similar paste called kashmiri masala is available from Indian grocers.

225g (8 oz) garlic cloves,	*25 large dry chillies, soaked*
peeled	*until soft and drained well*
450g (1 lb) fresh ginger, peeled	*2 teaspoons turmeric powder*
1 cup tightly packed coriander	*1 teaspoon fenugreek seeds,*
leaves and tender stems	*soaked overnight to swell*
4 teaspoons salt	*2 cups oil*

Grind all the ingredients in an electric blender, using oil to facilitate the blender. Grind to a smooth paste. Heat 1 cup oil in a heavy pan or a wok and when it has nearly reached smoking point add the ground paste and fry until the oil has separated from the mixture. Cool completely and store in airtight jars. As you have not used any liquid (water or vinegar, for example) and the paste is well fried, it will have a long larder life.

Deep-fried Onions

Deep-fried onions not only make a lovely garnish but have a delicious taste. I always have a batch in my larder.

*5 large onions, very finely
  sliced*

*oil for deep-frying
a little salt*

Heat sufficient oil for deep-frying in a wok or a deep frying pan. When it nearly reaches smoking point add the onions and fry until they are evenly brown in colour. In the last minute of frying sprinkle a little salt over the onions to make them crisp. Drain on sheets of newspaper, changing the newspaper once. Allow the onions to cool completely and then store in airtight jars.

COCONUT MILK

Many recipes require either thick or thin coconut milk. There are three ways of producing this, and I leave you to choose which one will suit you best.

Thick and Thin Coconut Milk from Fresh Coconuts

Break the shell, reserving the coconut water (delicious when chilled). Remove the brown skin and cut the coconut flesh into small pieces. Place in a blender and gradually liquidize the coconut flesh, adding a little ordinary milk or warm water.

Empty the contents into a large sieve and vigorously squeeze out as much thick milk as you can. Return the flesh to the blender and add the amount of water specified in the particular recipe you are using. Again, blend on a medium speed for 1–2 minutes. Empty the contents into the sieve, but squeeze out the thin milk into a separate bowl. If you have any milk left over, seal in an airtight plastic tumbler and either freeze it if you do not anticipate using it for a while, or keep it in the refrigerator for up to 4 days.

Thin coconut milk is usually added first during cooking and the thick milk is added during the last few minutes of cooking time. Once the thick milk had been added, stir constantly as it curdles easily. Do not cover the pan.

Thick and Thin Coconut Milk from Desiccated Coconut

Soak 1kg (2.2 lb) desiccated coconut in 300ml (½ pint) hot water for 1–2 hours, then transfer to a blender and liquidize on medium speed for 1–2 minutes. Empty the contents into a large sieve and squeeze out the thick coconut milk. This should produce about 230–285ml (6–8 fl oz). Return the coconut to the blender and add the amount of water specified in the recipe. Liquidize again for 1–2 minutes. Empty the contents into the sieve and squeeze out the thin coconut milk into a separate bowl.

Thick and Thin Coconut Milk from Creamed Coconut Blocks

Soak 75g (3 oz) chopped creamed coconut with a pinch of salt in 175ml (6 fl oz) hot water. Stir well until dissolved and then your thick milk is ready. For thin coconut milk, follow the same procedure but use only 25g (1 oz) creamed coconut. An alternative method is to soak 100g (4 oz) chopped creamed coconut in 350ml (12 fl oz) hot water with ½ teaspoon salt, stir until dissolved, and chill in the refrigerator. When it is fully chilled the cream will separate from the water and rise to the top. This can be spooned and used as the thick milk, and the remaining liquid can be used as the thin milk. Sometimes tinned coconut milk is available. Check the label carefully, because often it has been sweetened. Tinned coconut milk does not have a very thick consistency, so if you are using it add a little creamed coconut to complement it.

Tamarind Juice
(Imli pani)

Another ingredient regularly called for.

Soak a small fistful in 85ml (3 fl oz) hot water until pulpy and then vigorously squeeze out the juice through a fine sieve or a piece of muslin. If a recipe requires a larger quantity of tamarind juice, adjust the quantities accordingly.

Concentrated tamarind is now available from Chinese and Indian grocers. Follow the same method as above but use only 1 teaspoon of the concentrated pulp. I have recently come across bottled tamarind juice which can be used as it is in the quantity stated. Lemon juice or vinegar in roughly the same proportions can be used as a substitute, although these will not provide the cooling properties which tamarind has.

Planning Your Meal

You wake up in the morning. Your first thoughts are 'Oh god! What on earth shall I cook today?' Sounds familiar doesn't it? Precious time is lost each day wondering what to cook. Planning a menu that is both nutritious and palatable is an art in itself. The important point is to plan your menu in advance. I spend ten minutes each night before going to bed, planning the next day's menu, and, believe me, this method really works. Recipe books also make wonderful light reading before bedtime.

When planning a menu care should be taken not to end up with an ill-balanced, drab and monotonous selection. See that the food you are planning to prepare will not only be attractive and appetizing but also nutritionally well balanced. In India food habits are influenced to a great extent by educational and economic status, religious dogmas, custom and environment, superstitious beliefs, availability and family and personal likes and dislikes.

Ever since man has appeared on this earth he has been constantly endeavouring to meet his basic requirements for survival. Though hunger is satisfied with the ingestion of food the ultimate purpose of food is to meet the nutritional needs of the body. Planning meals for your family entails consideration of the individual members of the family. If you have to include children when planning a menu make sure you have borne in mind their taste. There is no joy obtained from 'force-feeding' any child. Provide satiety value in every meal. A satisfying meal is one which delays the onset of hunger, almost until the next meal.

Every meal should be centred round a main dish, one which is preferably rich in protein. Protein-rich sources are eggs, pulses and lentils. After deciding on the main dish, choose the cereal and vegetables to go with it. We are lucky to have a wide variety of cereal available to us, like wheat, rice, *bajara*, *jowar* and millet. If, for example, your cereal dish is wheat, don't be under the mistaken impression that you can only make chappatis with wheat. There is a wide variety to choose from including *pulkhas*, *rotis*, *baturas* and *parathas* (plain or stuffed). Similarly, rice can be served either plain, or in the form of *pilau*, *biryani* or, if you prefer, a combination with pulses, as in *kitchdi*.

Next come the vegetables to go with the cereal dish. A wide variety is available on the market and it is worth the trouble to look around. If possible include green leafy vegetables like fenugreek spinach or ordinary spinach because they are excellent sources of calcium and iron. Yellow vegetables are rich in vitamins. Even the same vegetable can be served in different interesting ways. For example, carrots can be served raw and grated for salads, boiled for a vegetable curry or in yogurt in the form of carrot *raitha* (see page 211).

Special attention should be applied to the texture of the food because this enhances appreciation of the food. Soft foods must be served soft and crisp foods must be served crisp. The temperature at which food is served improves the palatability of a meal: foods that are meant to be served hot should be piping hot, and foods meant to be served cold should be properly chilled. Choose appropriate garnishes for your dishes. Remember that garnishing always brings out the attractiveness of a dish. Be original in the use of colours. Sit for a few minutes and think hard, and you will be surprised at the flood of ideas that will come to you. With a little thought and imagination your meals are bound to win compliments!

Having planned your menu in advance, study the recipes carefully. Collect all the necessary ingredients or substitutes (in Indian cooking it is the preparation that takes the time). Once you have found all the ingredients, lay them in the order they are to be used. Keeping every article in order is a great time-saver. I keep all the containers labelled and arranged according to how frequently they will be used. Evolve a system when cooking – all the articles required for one preparation should be placed within easy reach near the stove to avoid unnecessary panic. Another effective time-saver is to make two things simultaneously. For example, if you are making a vegetable dish and chappatis, keep the vegetables and spices ready and then knead the flour for the chappatis. Keep the dough aside. Start cooking the vegetable dish and when you have to allow it to simmer start making your chappatis. This way you will be able to serve both dishes freshly made.

MENU SUGGESTIONS

When I am planning a menu I bear the following points in mind:
1. Choose either a bread or rice dish or both as vehicles for the main dishes.

2. Choose a green leafy vegetable dish to provide you with the vitamin requirement.
3. Choose a root or tuber dish for bulk food or an egg and cheese dish.
4. Choose a pulse dish to provide you with the protein requirement.
5. Choose an accompaniment from pickles, chutneys, *raithas* or salads.
6. Serve *papadums* whenever possible as these are enjoyed by all.
7. Choose a sweet dish or serve fresh fruit.
8. Serve several dishes and if you have more than 4–6 people dining add one extra dish per person rather than increasing quantities of ingredients as this will provide a wider selection. Indians tend to eat a little from several dishes rather than a lot from just one dish.

Simple Family Lunch or Dinner 1

Plain boiled rice　　　　*Any* raitha *or natural yogurt*
Spinach and potato　　　*Any chutney, pickle or salad*
Fried okra　　　　　　　*Quick mango ice cream or*
Spiced lentil curry　　　　　*fresh fruit*

Simple Family Lunch or Dinner 2

Unleavened flat bread　　*Any chutney, pickle or salad*
Dry potato　　　　　　　*Rice pudding*
Bengal gram with snake
*　gourd*

Informal Lunch or Dinner 1

Exotic vegetable rice　　*Goanese potatoes*
Cabbage cutlets　　　　*Onion salad*
Red gram curry　　　　*Cheese and yogurt dessert*
Stuffed aubergines

Informal Lunch or Dinner 2

*Sliced bread and plain flour
    bread or leavened bread*
Savoury chickpeas
*Cottage cheese with tomato
    gravy*

Vegetable raitha
Beetroot pudding

Formal Lunch or Dinner 1

Mango drink
Vegetable biryani
Tomato juice curry
Rich aubergine curry
Egg curry Rafi style

Cheese and spinach
Any chutney
Any pickle
Indian fruit salad
Dried apricot sweet

Formal Lunch or Dinner 2

Cumin water
Rice with gram or chickpeas
Brussels sprout curry
Cauliflower roast
Potato cutlets

Mushrooms and peas
Any chutney
Any pickle
Spongy cheese balls in syrup
Mango squash

Fun Menu

Puffed puris *with spiced water*
Bhelpuri
Batata puri

Aloo chat
Savoury doughnuts
Savoury biscuit (kachori)

Tea Party

Samosa
Savoury fritters
Banana fritters
Aubergine puffs
Doughnuts in yogurt

Cheese fries
*Spiced tea or tea and fruit
    punch*

South Indian Style Thali 1

Plain rice	*Natural yogurt or buttermilk*
Chappatis or puris	Papadums
Sambhar	*Pickles*
Onion and cabbage	*Ghee (to sprinkle over the*
Vegetable curry (kootu)	*rice)*
Rasam	*Banana*

South Indian Style Thali 2

South Indian vengi bhath	*Mango pickle*
Puris	*Green gram salad*
Aviyal	*Vermicelli pudding*
Red potatoes	*Spiced coffee*
Lentil curry with spinach	
Lime or tomato rasam	
Vegetable raitha	

Serving the Food

The Western style of eating is taking over the various Indian styles which have been part of our heritage and culture for centuries. The Hindus generally serve their meal on a *thali* – a large round metal plate. The rice, bread and dry dishes are placed on the *thali* and the curries and 'wet accompaniments', like yogurt, are served in *katories* – tiny bowls – placed along one edge of the *thali*. Alternatively, the meal is served on a well-washed banana leaf.

The Muslims serve their meal on a *dastar khan*. A white sheet is laid on a carpeted floor and the meal is served on this. The diners sit round the sheet and eat out of individual plates. On a festive occasion colourful cushions are scattered for the guests to recline on. Another Muslim way of serving food is on a very large round metal platter, large enough to seat 8–10 diners around it. The platter is placed on a *kundli* – a broad metal ring which acts as the table leg. Curries are placed in bowls in the centre of the platter and then a ring of rice is placed around them. Each diner draws the rice in front of him and then helps himself to the curry and accompaniment of his choice. Each diner is also provided with a small plate and a china spoon. The plate is used to place the inedible items and the spoon is used to sip curries with a liquid consistency. When a dish like Garlic Tops with Eggs is served in this manner, cinders are placed in the metal ring to keep the dish constantly hot.

Most Indian meals work around the rice or bread dish. Try each curry with a little rice or a bread dish. Do not mix everything. Trying out each curry individually not only gives you a variety of flavours but also shows appreciation to the cook who has spent a lot of time. Usually a bread dish with a dry curry is served first and then rice with one or two vegetable curries, a lentil curry accompanied with yogurt, pickles, chutneys and *papadums*. Some communities in India, like the Punjabis, Bengalis and some Muslims, start and end their meal with a sweet dish.

Traditionally Indians always eat with the fingers of their right hand only, the left hand being considered 'unclean'. With the exception of the south Indians, the food is delicately picked up with the tips of the fingers and placed in the mouth. The south Indians are very fond of *rasam* – spiced broth – and buttermilk and because these dishes are watery they pick it up in the palm of their right hand, which acts as a large spoon. But if you are not an expert you could dirty your whole hand. My brother took to using cutlery when he was very young and I remember my father ticking him off, saying that God gave us a spoon and a fork in the palm of our hands and that our hands were more hygienic than cutlery. My father is a large man with big hands, yet he eats so delicately that his fingers never get dirty beyond the first line on his palm.

Similar to Christians who say grace before eating, Muslims

commence their meal by saying '*Bis millah irrehma nir-rabeem*' – 'In the name of God most gracious, ever merciful' – and taking a pinch of salt. The Hindus, if eating in the traditional style sitting on the floor, will sprinkle some water round the *thali* or banana leaf. The circle of water acts as a barrier to any evil. A small prayer is said before the dining commences. If they are dining from a banana leaf this is neatly folded up and then discarded when the meal is over. It's a wonderful way of eating and a housewife's washing up is reduced considerably.

Some golden Indian tips about eating:

1. Ensure your kitchen is hygienically clean and keep all food articles covered to avoid exposure.
2. Eat only when you are hungry.
3. Wash your hands before eating, even if you are using cutlery.
4. If possible, eat with your fingers.
5. Before you eat say a small prayer. This will also help your mind to relax. Then take a sip of water or taste a pinch of salt to refresh your mouth.
6. Eat in a bright room and listen to light music. This will keep you cheerful.
7. Leave the table when you still have some desire to eat.
8. Before leaving the table say a small prayer of thanks.
9. Whenever possible continue to relax for a while after your food.
10. Eat wisely and be healthy.
11. LIVE NOT TO EAT, BUT EAT TO LIVE – you are what you eat.

'*Sanjog Bhojan*' – 'Happy dining'.

Breakfast and Snack-time Dishes

Indian regional snacks are truly a gourmet's delight. The range is so vast that a complete book could be written about them, and the task of selecting the few in this chapter was very difficult.

Indians are great lovers of titbits, anywhere and at any time of the day. Dishes like *dosai*, *idlis*, *vadai* and *uppama* were once only served as breakfast dishes, and housewives rose early to prepare these before sending their husbands off to work and children to school. Now they are served all day long and you can pop in to any restaurant serving these dishes when you feel peckish. When I was dating my boyfriend, now my husband, in Madras in the early sixties, we often ate these dishes as they are cheap yet substantial.

Pancakes
Dosai
Makes 8–10

These are the famous south Indian pancakes made from fermented batter. There are several varieties and it was difficult to decide which was my favourite. I hope you will like my choice.

½ cup black gram (urad dhal)   salt to taste
1 cup patna or long-grain   ghee or oil for frying
   rice

Soak the *dhal* and the rice separately in water for about 8 hours or preferably overnight. Drain the *dhal* and reserve the water. Drain the rice. In an electric blender grind them separately until you have a smooth paste. Use the *dhal* water to lubricate the blender. Mix the pastes together and add some *dhal* water so you have a batter of pouring consistency. Cover the bowl with a kitchen towel and leave in a warm place overnight to ferment. As a result of fermentation the ground paste increases in volume. So, to avoid spilling use a bowl which will allow for this increase. If, the next day, the batter has become too thick add some more water. Heat a heavy flat griddle or a *tava* and brush it with ghee or oil. Pour a ladleful of the batter on to it, spreading it out thinly with the back of the ladle, using circular movements. Cover with a lid. When the edges begin to shrink put a teaspoon of ghee or oil around the *dosa* (pancake) and gently ease it off with a flat spatula. Turn the *dosa* and cook on the other side. Make sure the griddle is piping hot and that once you have poured the batter you work fast. If you make them a while before serving, wrap them in a kitchen towel or a sheet of foil. Serve hot with either *aloo sag* (page 164) or *sambhar* (page 186) and *nariyal* chutney (page 242). Or try it on its own with an extra dab of ghee and sugar.

Fluffy Rice Cakes
Idlis
Makes 20–24

Traditionally these delicious south Indian rice cakes were steamed by using muslin cloth or banana leaves. Now India has special *idli* receptacles, which are also available at some large Indian stockists in the UK. Alternatively, use a non-stick egg poacher.

3 cups patna or long-grain
   rice

1½ cups black gram (urad
   dhal)

salt to taste
a pinch soda bicarbonate
6 tablespoons oil

Soak the rice and *dhal* separately in water for about 4–6 hours.
In an electric blender grind the rice and *dhal* separately using
the *dhal* water to facilitate the blending. Grind both the rice
and *dhal* to a fine paste. Mix the pastes and leave covered for 8
hours or overnight. The mixture should have the consistency
of double cream. Add salt to taste, soda bicarbonate and 2
tablespoons oil. Oil the depressions of an *idli* tray or egg
poaching pan. Pour a spoonful of the mixture into each
depression and steam for 10 minutes. Serve hot with *sambhar*
(page 186) and *nariyal* chutney (page 242).

Spiced Fluffy Rice Cakes
Masala Idlis
Makes 20–24

Use the same ingredients as for the previous recipe but add
the following to the ground paste.

1 onion, finely chopped
2 green chillies, finely chopped
a handful chopped coriander
   leaves

a pinch of asafoetida
a dash freshly ground black
   pepper

Savoury Doughnuts
Vadai
Makes 10–12

This is another traditionally south Indian dish of which there are several versions. It is a very popular snack sold at roadsides, on trains and buses. They are wrapped in banana leaves with coconut chutney and always enjoyed on train and bus journeys with hot, sweet tea.

1 cup plain flour, sieved
110ml (4 fl oz) natural yogurt
2 medium-sized onions, finely chopped
5-cm (2-inch) piece fresh ginger, finely crushed
4 green chillies, finely chopped
a few curry leaves, finely chopped
¼ teaspoon freshly ground black pepper
1 teaspoon desiccated coconut
a pinch cumin seeds
salt to taste
oil for deep-frying

Mix all the ingredients except the oil. Use an electric whisk as this will lighten the batter. Heat oil in a wok or a deep frying pan until nearly smoking. Reduce heat. Drop spoonfuls of the mixture and fry until the *vadai* are golden brown in colour. Do not fry too many at a time. Serve hot with *sambhar* (page 186) and *nariyal* chutney (page 242) or just some tomato ketchup mixed with a little chilli sauce.

Doughnuts in Yogurt
Dahi Vadai
Makes 10–12

In most Indian homes *dahi* (natural yogurt) forms part of every meal. It is a nourishing food with the added advantage of having a high nutritional value combined with a low calorie content. It is easily digested and can be served in such a wide variety of ways that it is virtually impossible to imagine a meal without *dahi* in one form or another. This dish is a popular one from Punjab, and can be prepared in advance. Serve it as a snack, at buffets or as a starter.

FOR THE DOUGHNUTS

2 cups black gram (urad dhal), *soaked in water for 24 hours*

3 green chillies, finely chopped

4 tablespoons desiccated coconut

15 raisins

a handful coriander leaves, chopped

¼ teaspoon baking powder

salt to taste

oil for deep-frying

FOR THE YOGURT

450ml (¾ pint) natural yogurt, well beaten

salt to taste

2 tablespoons oil

½ teaspoon cumin seeds

2 dried red chillies

FOR THE CHUTNEY

a fistful tamarind

6 preserved dates, ground to paste

1 teaspoon freshly ground coriander powder

light brown sugar to taste

a few coriander leaves to garnish

Drain the *dhal* well and grind to a smooth paste in an electric blender, using the least amount of water as possible to facilitate the blending. Add the chillies, coconut, raisins, coriander leaves, baking powder and salt and mix well. Divide into 10–12 equal portions. Grease the palm of your hand and make a flat round and then make a hole in the centre. Heat oil for deep-frying until nearly smoking. Reduce heat and fry the *vadai* until golden brown in colour. Drain well and put the *vadai* in hot water for about 10 minutes. Remove *vadai* from the water and squeeze out as much water as possible without breaking them. Leave them on a piece of cloth to drain for a few minutes. Arrange *vadai* in a shallow serving dish.

Heat 2 tablespoons oil and fry the cumin seeds and chillies until fragrant. Pour the oil and spices on the beaten yogurt. Add salt to taste and mix well. Pour the yogurt over the *vadai*.

Soak the tamarind in a cup of boiling water. When soft squeeze out the juice through a fine sieve. Mix in the dates, coriander powder and sugar to taste. Garnish with coriander leaves. Serve the *vadai* and chutney separately, allowing the diners to help themselves. *Vadai* can also be fried and served with tomato ketchup.

Savoury Semolina

Uppama

Serves 4–6

A wholesome and tasty snack, mostly prepared by the south Indians. This is how it is prepared in the state of Andhra Pradesh where I grew up. Try it at a coffee morning. Use 225g (8 oz) bulgar instead of semolina for a coarser texture.

225g (8 oz) semolina
25g (1 oz) butter or ghee
3 tablespoons oil
1 teaspoon mustard seeds
50g (2 oz) cashew nuts
2 large onions, chopped
a handful coriander leaves,
*   chopped*

300ml (½ pint) water
2 green chillies, chopped
½ teaspoon ground
*   cinnamon*
½ teaspoon ground cloves
juice of 2 lemons
salt to taste

Heat a large frying pan and dry-roast the semolina until brown, then set aside. Heat the butter or ghee and oil in a large pan and fry mustard seeds until they crackle. Add the cashew nuts and fry for 1 minute. Add the onions and coriander leaves and fry until the onions are soft and translucent. Add half the water and the remaining ingredients except the semolina. Bring to the boil and simmer for 5 minutes. Gradually fold in the semolina stirring constantly. Add the remaining water and mix well. Cover the pan with a tight-fitting lid and allow to simmer until the mixture dries out and leaves the sides of the pan. Serve hot with mango pickle. I also like the way the Andhra people have it, with sugar sprinkled on it.

Bulgar with Tamarind
Bulgar Puliotharai

Bulgar is rich in protein and phosphorous: 100g (4 oz) provides 356 calories. This dish can be eaten as a snack with a tossed green salad, or as a main dish with a leafy vegetable dish and a lentil curry.

400g (14 oz) bulgar
6 cups water
2 tablespoons sesame oil
½ teaspoon mustard seeds
½ teaspoon cumin seeds

½ teaspoon turmeric powder
50g (2 oz) raw peanuts
50g (2 oz) cashew nuts
6 tablespoons tamarind juice
salt to taste

Ingredients to be dry-roasted and ground
*1 teaspoon black gram (*urad dhal*)*
1 teaspoon bengal gram (channa dhal)
a pinch asafoetida
5 green chillies

1 tablespoon sesame seeds
2 tablespoons coriander seeds
8 peppercorns
a few curry leaves

Cook the bulgar in water until soft. Drain and set aside,

reserving the water. Heat oil in a large pan and fry the mustard seeds and cumin seeds until the mustard seeds crackle. Add the turmeric powder and the ground ingredients. Reduce heat and fry for 2 minutes. Add the nuts and fry for another 2 minutes. Add the tamarind juice and 4 tablespoons reserved water. Simmer for 5 minutes. Gradually fold in the cooked bulgar and mix well. Cover the pan with a tight-fitting lid and allow to simmer for 5 minutes. Serve hot.

The following four recipes are famous snacks from Maharashtra and Gujerat. Along the coast of Bombay these are sold at colourful stalls on the beaches and cost very little. Today crockery and cutlery are used to eat them but I enjoyed these more when they were served on banana leaves. *Pani puri* is the difficult one. My mouth is rather small and trying to eat whole *puri* filled with spiced water is always a challenge. These are fun dishes, so why not try them at a garden party? Very little cooking is required. Keep the crisp ingredients separate and add just before serving. I lay out all the ingredients separately and then mix them together for each person, leaving them to add the chutney. The preparations can be done well in advance so you can be relaxed and cheerful when serving.

Each recipe serves 4–6 but if you provide all four snacks they should serve 8–10.

Puffed Puris with Spiced Water
Pani Puri

FOR SPICED WATER

*1 cup whole green gram
  (mung)
1.2 litres (2 pints) water
110ml (4 fl oz) tamarind
juice
1 bunch coriander leaves,
  chopped*

*1 teaspoon chilli powder
1 teaspoon cumin powder
½ teaspoon freshly ground
  black pepper
jaggery or demerara sugar to
  taste
salt to taste*

Soak the green gram overnight. Next day boil them until tender. Drain and set aside, reserving the water. If the water has reduced in quantity add some more to make up 1.2 litres (2 pints). Add the remaining ingredients except the green gram and bring to the boil. Simmer until the jaggery or sugar has dissolved. Cool compeltely and serve green gram and spiced water in separate bowls.

FOR PURIS

*450g (1 lb) plain flour
1 teaspoon salt*

oil for deep-frying

Sieve the flour and salt. Add enough water to make a stiff dough. Roll out thin sheets of pastry and cut with a circular cutter the size of a 50p piece. Heat enough oil for deep-frying and when nearly smoking fry a few *puris* at a time until they puff and are golden brown in colour. (Any *puris* that do not puff can be used in the next two recipes.) Drain well and carefully store them, ensuring you do not break them. To serve ask each individual to take a *puri* and make a hole in one side. Place a little green gram in the *puri* and then fill the *puri* with spiced water. Now open your mouth wide and pop the whole *puri* in and relish this lovely snack.

The next three dishes also require *puris*. Follow the same

method as for *pani puri* but roll out the pastry a little thicker before cutting. Deep-fry them but do not encourage them to puff out. Drain well and set aside.

The accompanying chutneys for these dishes are also the same.

SWEET CHUTNEY

100g (4 oz) tamarind
225g (8 oz) jaggery or light brown sugar
1 bunch coriander leaves, chopped

1 teaspoon chilli powder
1 teaspoon coriander powder
1 teaspoon fennel powder
1 teaspoon cumin powder
a pinch salt

Soak the tamarind in 2 cups of boiling water. When the tamarind has softened vigorously strain the juice through a fine sieve. Add the remaining ingredients and mix well. The chutney should have the consistency of single cream, so dilute with more water accordingly. Serve in a small bowl.

HOT CHUTNEY

1 bunch coriander leaves
1 cup tightly packed mint leaves
6 green chillies
1 teaspoon chilli powder
½ teaspoon cumin powder
a pinch asafoetida

2 teaspoons amchur *(dry mango powder)*
juice of 1 lemon (if you cannot get amchur *powder increase to 2 lemons)*
salt to taste

Grind all the ingredients, using the lemon juice to facilitate the blending. Serve in a small bowl.

Bhel Puri

Puffed rice (*murmura*) is available from Indian grocers. If you cannot obtain this use unsugared roasted rice cereal. *Sev-ghatia* is available from Indian grocers and can often be found in health food shops and sometimes even in supermarkets.

100g (4 oz) puffed rice
  (murmura)
50g (2 oz) fine sev ghatia
12 puris *(page 76), coarsely*
  broken
1 onion, finely chopped

1 large potato, boiled, peeled
  and diced
a handful coriander leaves,
  chopped
1 teaspoon garam masala
salt to taste

Toss all the ingredients together. To serve allow each individual to help themselves and add their choice of chutney before eating. I like to have some of both chutneys.

Batata Puri

1 teaspoon cumin powder
a pinch chilli powder
a handful coriander leaves,
  chopped
6 potatoes, boiled, peeled and
  cut into small pieces

salt to taste
24 flat puris *(page 76)*
1 small carton natural
  yogurt, beaten
50g (2 oz) fine sev ghatia

Add the cumin powder. chilli powder and chopped coriander leaves to the potatoes, and salt to taste. Mix well. Serve *puris*, potatoes and yogurt in separate bowls. Allow each individual to take a *puri*, place some potato on it and then add a little yogurt and chutney of their choice before eating.

Aloo Chat

225g (8 oz) potatoes, boiled,
  peeled and diced
1 onion, finely chopped
4 green chillies, chopped
1 teaspoon chilli powder
1 teaspoon garam masala

1 teaspoon cumin powder
juice of 2 lemons
salt and sugar to taste
12 puris (page 76), coarsely
  broken

Toss all the ingredients. Eat with either sweet or hot chutney or a combination.

Samosas

Makes 24

One of India's most delicious snacks. Traditional *samosas* require a lot of time and hard work, so I have given you both the traditional method and a simple variation. To make perfect traditional *samosas* you have to be an artist with a lot of patience. When you have prepared the *samosas* they can be frozen before frying them. To serve frozen *samosas*, thaw them a little and then fry them using the method given below. They are handy to have in the freezer to serve as a quick snack to unexpected guests.

FOR FILLING

2 tablespoons oil
1 large onion, finely chopped
1 teaspoon coriander powder
1 teaspoon cumin powder
½ teaspoon turmeric powder
½ teaspoon chilli powder or
  2 green chillies, finely
  chopped
¼ teaspoon omum (ajwain),
  optional

2.5cm (1-inch) fresh ginger,
  finely chopped
a handful coriander leaves,
  finely chopped
salt to taste
a pinch sugar
4 large potatoes, boiled,
  peeled and coarsely
  mashed
juice of 2 lemons

Heat oil and fry the onion until soft and translucent. Add the remaining ingredients except the potato and lemon juice. Sprinkle a little water and cook for 5 minutes, or until the water has evaporated. Fold in the potato and mix well. Remove from the heat and add the lemon juice and again mix well. Allow mixture to cool before filling the *samosas*.

Traditional Samosas

350g (12 oz) plain flour
½ teaspoon salt

tepid water
ghee or oil

Sieve the flour and salt. Make a well and add a little water at a time, then knead well until you have gathered all the dry flour and made a stiff dough. Divide into 48 equal portions. Make them into flat cakes. Take a pair at a time and put a little ghee or oil in between. Roll each pair out as thinly as possible. When you have rolled out all the pairs heat a *tava* or heavy griddle and roast each pair of rolled pastry for 1 minute on each side.

Carefully separate the two layers and cut them into strips about 5cm (2 inches) wide and 18cm (7 inches) long. Cover the strips with a damp cloth while you are filling them.

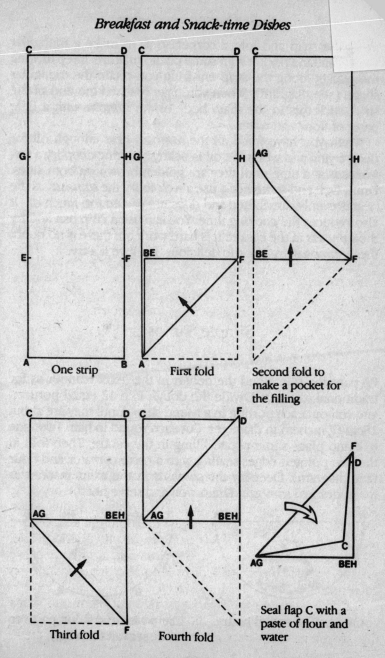

One strip

First fold

Second fold to
make a pocket for
the filling

Third fold

Fourth fold

Seal flap C with a
paste of flour and
water

Take one strip and fold a corner so as to make a triangular pocket. Fill the pocket with some potato mixture. Keep turning the pocket along the strip ensuring you retain the triangular shape (see diagram). When you have reached the end of the strip, stick this to the main body of the *samosa* with a little paste of flour and water.

When you have filled all the *samosas* heat enough oil for deep-frying and when the oil is nearly smoking deep-fry a few *samosas* at a time until they are golden brown on both sides. Drain well and serve hot. I use a wok to fry the *samosas* as the heat is evenly distributed and does not use up too much oil. It also reduces the cooking time. You can use a chip pan and fry the *samosas* in the basket. It is hard work but there is no doubt these *samosas* are just too delicious. Do give it a try.

Simple Samosas

Prepare the filling and the dough in the exact manner as for traditional *samosas*. Divide the dough into 12 equal portions and roll out each portion in a round shape until they are about 18cm (7 inches) in diameter. Cut each round in half. Take one half and place some potato filling in the centre. Then fold in the two pointed edges sealing with a paste of water and flour (see diagram). Deep-fry the *samosas* in the exact manner as for traditional *samosas*. Drain well and serve hot.

One half of rolled pastry.

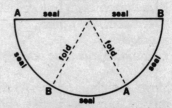

Use water and flour paste to seal all the edges.

 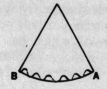

Either make a decorative pattern by using the back of the fork tip, or by pinching edge with your thumb and finger.

Savoury Fritters
Bhajias
Serves 4–6

Bhajias are an established classic snack in India. They can be served at formal parties, cocktail parties or even as an hors d'oeuvre. You can make *bhajias* with almost any vegetable and some are also made with pulses and nuts. When using vegetables the batter is standard but each variety will have its own distinctive flavour.

BATTER

225g (8 oz) gram flour (besan or channa atta)
½ teaspoon chilli powder
½ teaspoon coriander powder
1 teaspoon turmeric powder

1 teaspoon baking powder
salt to taste
2 green chillies, finely chopped
a few coriander leaves, finely chopped

Sieve the flour, spices, baking powder and salt in a large mixing bowl. Add the chillies and coriander leaves. Add sufficient water to make a fairly thick batter. The batter should be thick enough to coat approximately 225–350g (8–12 oz) vegetables before frying. Either make a selection of *bhajias* or if you prefer use only one vegetable. *Bhajias* should be deep-fried in oil which has been fairly well pre-heated. Under-heated oil makes *bhajias* greasy and soggy.

Here is a selection of *bhajias*:

Potato 1

Boil the potatoes until nearly cooked. Peel and cut into slices 6mm (¼ inch) thick. Dip individual slices in the batter and coat well. Deep-fry in hot oil until golden brown on both sides. Drain well and serve hot.

Potato 2

Boil, peel and mash the potatoes. Add 1 chopped onion, 1 chopped green chilli, a few chopped coriander leaves, a pinch of turmeric, salt to taste and a little lemon juice. Mix well. Make balls and cover them individually with the batter and deep-fry until golden brown. Drain well and serve hot.

Onion 1

Peel and cut the onions into rings 12mm (½ inch) thick. Dip each ring individually in the batter and coat well. Deep-fry in hot oil until golden brown on both sides. Drain well and serve hot.

Onion 2

Peel and chop the onions coarsely. Mix into the batter. Drop spoonfuls of the mixture into hot oil and fry until they are golden brown on all sides. Do not overcrowd the pan and leave sufficient space in between to allow for turning. Drain well and serve hot.

Spinach

Clean, wash and dry the leaves. Dip individual leaves in batter and deep-fry in hot oil until golden brown on both sides. Drain well and serve hot.

Aubergine

Cut into rings 6mm (¼ inch) thick. Soak in water if you are

not using them immediately. Drain and dry the rings. Dip individual rings in the batter and deep-fry in hot oil until golden brown on both sides. Drain well and serve hot.

Cauliflower

Cut into florets. You can leave them raw or parboil them. Drain well. Dip each individual floret in the batter and deep-fry in hot oil until golden brown on all sides. Drain well and serve hot.

Large green chillies

Wash and dry them thoroughly. Seed them for a milder flavour. Leave stalk on if possible. Dip individual chilli and coat well in the batter. Deep-fry in hot oil until golden brown on all sides. Drain well and serve hot.

Peppers – green, yellow or red

Cut into large pieces. Dip individual pieces in the batter and coat well. Deep-fry in hot oil until golden brown on both sides. Drain well and serve hot.

Fenugreek

Break leaves, wash and drain well. Mix in the batter. Drop spoonfuls of the mixture in hot oil and fry until golden brown on all sides. Drain well and serve hot.

Cashew nuts

Mix raw cashew nuts in the batter and drop spoonfuls into hot oil and fry until golden brown on all sides. Drain well and serve either hot or cold.

Grated coconut

Mix 1 freshly grated coconut in the batter and drop spoonfuls into hot oil. Fry until golden brown on all sides. Drain well and serve hot.

You can also use marrow, courgettes, sweet potato and okra. For marrow and courgettes follow the procedure for aubergine. For sweet potato follow the ordinary potato method 1 or 2. For okra just wash and dry them but leave them whole.

The batter can be made into plain *bhajias* without the addition of any vegetables. In this case make the batter a little thicker.

If you drop the batter through a slotted spoon on to hot oil you will obtain *boondis* – small tear-shaped *bhajias*. Fry them quickly and then drain well. Serve mixed with natural yogurt as a *raitha*.

Moong Dhal (Green Gram) *Bhajias*

Serves 4–6

1 cup moong dhal *(split)*
1 medium-sized onion, chopped
1 teaspoon baking powder
salt to taste
1 teaspoon coriander powder

1 green chilli, finely chopped
¼ teaspoon chilli powder (optional)
a few coriander leaves, chopped
1 egg

Wash *dhal* and soak overnight. Drain well and grind to a smooth paste in a blender. Remove from the blender and fold in the remaining ingredients. If this batter is too watery add a little plain flour or gram flour to obtain a dropping consistency. Mould with hands into cutlets and fry in deep hot oil until dark brown. Drain well. Serve hot or cold.

Bombay Mix
Chevda

Once a popular Gujerati snack, this is now enjoyed all over India. If you are making a large batch it will store well in an airtight jar. A lovely titbit to accompany drinks instead of the usual peanuts and crisps. Beaten rice, known as *chevda* or *poha*, is available from Indian grocers but if you cannot obtain this use roasted rice cereal.

150g (5 oz) beaten rice
1 large packet ready salted finger crisps
50g (2 oz) bengal gram (channa dhal), *soaked overnight*
25g (1 oz) dry coconut slices (copra), *also available from healthfood shops*
6 green chillies, seeded and cut in large pieces
a few curry leaves

1 tablespoon cumin seeds, dry-roasted
25g (1 oz) fried peanuts with the skin
25g (1 oz) fried cashew nuts
25g (1 oz) fried raisins
1 tablespoon turmeric powder
1 tablespoon sugar
¼ teaspoon garam masala
salt and chilli powder to taste

Deep-fry the beaten rice until golden brown. Drain well and cool. Mix in the finger crisps. Drain the bengal gram well and deep-fry to a golden brown. Drain well, cool and add to the rice. Fry the coconut slices until golden brown. Drain well, cool and add to the rice. Fry the green chillies and curry leaves until crisp and golden. Drain well, cool and add to the rice. Mix in the remaining ingredients. Cool thoroughly and store in airtight jars.

Ready-made packets of *chevda* are now easily available but making up a batch yourself works out more economical.

Crispy Bengal Gram
Channa Zor Garam

An Indian film made this snack very popular when they used its name in a song sequence. Along the beaches of Bombay you find hawkers selling this delicious snack humming the song, 'Chana zor garam mai laya mazedar, babu chana zor garam' – 'Sir, I have brought you these delicious grams, please buy them.'

450g (1 lb) bengal gram
  (channa dhal) – *left whole*
2 dessertspoons chilli powder
1 dessertspoon coriander
  seeds

½ dessertspoon cumin seeds
1 teaspoon amchur (dry
  mango powder)
salt to taste
a little ghee or oil

Soak the bengal gram overnight then boil them until you can press them between your thumb and finger. Place the gram in a sieve and completely drain off the water. Place them on a chopping board and with a rolling pin lightly press the gram to form flat rounds without breaking them. Dry-roast the coriander seeds and cumin seeds and then grind them to a fine powder and mix with the chilli powder, dry mango powder and salt.

Heat a little oil or ghee in a *karai* or a wok and fry the flattened gram in it carefully so as not to break them. Fry them until they are crisp and dry. Remove from the heat and fold in the ground spices. Toss well. Serve hot, or leave to cool completely and store in airtight jars.

You can also use peanuts and cashew nuts but do not crush them.

Aubergine Puffs
Baingan Pakoras
Serves 4–6

Naughty, I am. I serve this at drinks parties and my guests try them thinking they are ordinary fritters. I love disguising Indian dishes with Western ideas. My guests have no complaints and I have no leftovers.

*3 long dark purple
   aubergines
6 cloves garlic, ground to a
   paste
2.5-cm (1-inch) piece fresh
   ginger, ground to a paste
1 tablespoon ghee or
   unsalted butter
8 tablespoons grated cheese*

*1 potato, boiled, peeled and
   mashed
2 tablespoons butter
1 egg
4 tablespoons plain flour
milk to make a batter
salt and pepper to taste
oil for deep-frying*

Slice the aubergines into rounds about 6mm (¼ inch) thick. Mix the garlic and ginger pastes and apply to the slices of aubergines. Heat a wok (preferably a non-stick one) or a large non-stick frying pan and melt the ghee or unsalted butter and sauté the aubergine slices on both sides for a few minutes. Keep aside. Mix the cheese, potato and butter and spread this mixture between two slices of aubergine to make sandwiches. Beat the egg and flour adding milk gradually to make a thick batter. Add salt and pepper to taste. Dip the pairs of aubergine in this batter and deep-fry them in piping hot oil until evenly brown and crisp. Drain well and serve hot. Serve with the cheese dip (page 219) or tomato ketchup.

There will be some bits of aubergine which you will not be able to match into pairs. Leave these to soak in water and they will keep fresh in a refrigerator for a few days. You can use these in a mixed vegetable dish or in a lentil curry.

Jaggery Biscuits
Theplas
Serves 4–6

Another favourite of the north Indians. I regret that there is no substitute for jaggery in this recipe, but it is easily available from Indian grocers.

2 cups wholemeal flour or
    wheat flour (atta)
1 teaspoon grated nutmeg

1½ cups melted ghee
1 cup grated jaggery
oil for deep-frying

Sieve the flour with the nutmeg in a large mixing bowl. Add the ghee and jaggery and make a firm dough. Leave to stand for three hours. Knead the dough again for a few minutes and then roll out the pastry to 6mm (¼ inch) thickness. Cut into desired shapes. Heat enough oil for deep-frying and over a medium heat fry the biscuits until they are golden brown and crisp. Drain well and cool thoroughly before storing.

Savoury Biscuits
Kachoris

A delicious snack from the state of Bihar. They can be eaten on their own or as suggested below.

250g (9 oz) plain flour
salt to taste
¼ teaspoon chilli powder
½ teaspoon ginger powder
50g (2 oz) melted ghee
100g (4 oz) black gram (urad
    dhal), soaked overnight

1 teaspoon coarsely pounded
    cumin seeds
1 teaspoon coarsely pounded
    coriander seeds

Sieve the flour, salt, chilli powder and ginger powder. Rub in the ghee and add enough water to make a pliable dough. Leave aside for 30 minutes. Drain the *dhal* thoroughly, place on a chopping board and coarsely crush with a rolling pin. Collect the *dhal* in a bowl and season with salt and pepper. Knead the dough for a few minutes and then divide into equal portions the size of golf balls. Shape into balls and then flatten them. In the centre of each place some of the *dhal* and seal them by folding in the dough. Heat enough oil for deep-frying and when the oil is nearly smoking hot reduce the heat to medium and deep-fry the *kachoris* until they are golden brown and crisp. Drain well and serve hot or cold. They will store for up to 15 days in an airtight container.

When we eat them in India, we knock a hole in the centre of each *kachori* and fill it up with either sweet or hot chutney (page 77), then put beaten yogurt over them before serving.

Puffed Rice Toffee
Murmura Chikki
Serves 4—6

A variety of homemade toffees are produced in India. On the train journey between Poona and Bombay when we are climbing the exciting *ghats* the train moves slowly and young boys and girls jump on with baskets filled with these delicious toffees which they are selling.

25g (1 oz) butter	*2 cups puffed rice* (murmura)
225g (8 oz) jaggery	*or roasted rice cereal*
1 teaspoon lemon juice	

Melt the butter with jaggery and lemon juice over a low heat. Stir well. Test the consistency by dropping a little drop in cold water. If it does not disintegrate it is ready. Remove from the heat and quickly but gently fold in the puffed rice. Empty on to a greased tray and cut into desired shapes while still warm. Allow to cool completely before easing the pieces off from the tray. Store in a cool place.

Alternatively, you can use 1 cup roasted peanuts, coarsely crushed or 1½ cups toasted sesame seeds. When using peanuts and sesame seeds these should be added while the syrup is still on the fire, stirred well and then removed and levelled out into a greased tray. These should also be cut into desired shapes while still warm.

Rice

In India rice is consumed by the poor and the rich. There are numerous ways in which it can be prepared and plain boiled rice is the most common. Then we have *kitchdi* (rice cooked with lentils). In India there is a classic joke about this dish. When one serves it to house guests who have overstayed their welcome it is a polite hint that they should start packing. Nevertheless, *kitchdis* are enjoyed by all. *Pilaus* and *biryanis* were introduced to us by the Moghuls. *Pilaus* do not require the same intricate method as *biryanis* and I remember with nostalgia the days when my grandmother used to make them. She took a great deal of pride and care in them and all the servants were sworn to secrecy. She generally prepared non-vegetarian *biryanis* but I follow her method for a vegetarian *biryani*. Although I must confess I do not seal the pan with dough or weigh the lid down with live embers or a hot brick, I do abide by her one important rule — never open a pan while the *biryani* is cooking. To check if it is cooked place one end of a hollow bamboo at the base of the pan and listen through it. If there is no sizzling sound from inside the pan the *biryani* is done. Alternatively, sprinkle some cold water on the outside wall of the pan; if it sizzles away quickly the *biryani* is done. *Biryani* always announces itself by emitting the most engulfing aroma and I am sure it will make even the most fastidious smack their lips in anticipation. I have given my favourite vegetable *biryani* recipe but you can use the vegetable of your own choice.

Plain Boiled Rice

U: *Khushka*   H: *Saday Chawal*   T: *Sadam*

Rice originally travels in large gunny sacks and often faces a long journey before being neatly packaged for commercial purposes. So, whatever quality rice you use, it should be thoroughly washed before cooking — although I do realize that this decreases its nutritional value.

I usually follow this measuring method and I can assure you it has never failed me.

1 cup rice + 1½ cups water = 2 persons
2 cups rice + 3 cups water = 4 persons
3 cups rice + 4½ cups water = 6 persons

and so on.

The most important thing to remember is to measure the rice and the water with the same cup.

There are several ways of cooking rice perfectly, but I find this method the easiest, and it also preserves the vitamins and minerals which have remained after dehusking.

Serves 4

2 cups patna or long-grain
rice
3 cups water

a knob butter or a few drops
oil (I use olive oil)
½ teaspoon salt

Wash the rice in three or four changes of water or until the water remains clear. Refresh the water and soak the rice for about 20 minutes as this will give you a better yield when cooked. Drain the rice thoroughly and place in a pan with a tight-fitting lid. Measure the water and add to the rice along with the butter and salt. Bring to the boil and immediately reduce the heat to the lowest setting and cover the pan. Allow to simmer for about 20 minutes. Peek in to see if there are steam holes on the surface of the rice. If there are, the rice is cooked. Turn off the heat, replace the lid and allow the rice to rest for about 5 minutes before serving. When serving remove the rice in sections by pushing a flat spoon right down to the base of the pan instead of scraping it out in layers. Once you have transferred the rice to a serving platter gently loosen the grains. Serve plain or garnish with fried onion flakes (see page 58) or chopped coriander leaves or fried cashew nuts and raisins, or choose a garnish of your own.

Notes

1. If your pan does not have a tight-fitting lid first cover with a sheet of foil and then with the lid. This ensures there is no loss of the essential steam required to cook the rice.

2. If you only have an electric cooker bring the rice to the boil on a fully heated ring keeping a second ring on the lowest setting. As soon as the rice reaches a boil transfer it to the second ring and cover it immediately.

3. If you have any rice left over this will keep in a refrigerator for 2 or 3 days. To reheat it, place it in a sieve and steam it with a lid on. Leftover rice reheats beautifully in a microwave. Just place it in a dish and cover it. Follow the instructions on your microwave and heat according to the number of minutes recommended.

Leftover rice can also be frozen. To serve, thaw the rice at room temperature and steam, or defrost in a microwave and heat as above.

Spiced Rice
Bagare Chawal
Serves 4−6

Although rice has a delicious aroma of its own, the spices used in this recipe enhance it admirably. There are many variations but this recipe is my favourite, and a favourite also of north and Deccani Indians. Use basmati rice, which is now readily available at many supermarkets.

2 cups basmati rice
1 tablespoon ghee or oil
1 medium-sized onion, very finely sliced
½ teaspoon black cumin seeds (shahjeera)
1 cardamom, bruised

2.5-cm (1-inch) cinnamon quill
1 clove
1 teaspoon brown sugar
3 cups water
a pinch salt

Wash the rice thoroughly but gently as basmati rice grains are delicate. Leave to soak for 20 minutes. Heat the ghee or oil in a pan which has a tight-fitting lid. Fry the onions, cumin, cardamom, cinnamon and clove until the onions are golden brown. Add the sugar and fry until it caramelizes. Drain the rice well and add to the pan. Sauté the rice for a few minutes. Add the water and salt and bring to the boil. When it has reached the boil, reduce the heat to the lowest setting, cover the pan and leave to simmer for about 15–20 minutes. Follow the same hints I have given in the previous recipe. Serve hot.

Spiced rice is delicious with a lentil curry (page 179–80) and kebabs (page 126 and page 140), and can also be frozen. Follow the same instructions as for plain boiled rice (page 96).

Simple Rice with Lentils
Sadee Kitchdi
Serves 2–4

When I was touring India in 1984, my English friend Rosamund joined me for three weeks. On the fourth day she suffered from 'Delhi Belly'. I suggested that for twenty-four

hours she only had arrowroot water and the first n
that was a light *kitchdi* with natural yogurt. It worked ~~wonders~~
and she thoroughly enjoyed her supper and the rest of the
holiday.

½ cup red lentils (masoor
   dhal), *picked and washed*
½ teaspoon turmeric powder
2¼ cups water
*1 cup patna rice, picked and
   thoroughly washed*

salt to taste
2 teaspoons ghee
1 small onion, finely chopped
1 clove garlic, crushed

Cook the *dhal* with turmeric in 1 cup water. Simmer until the
dhal is half done. Drain the rice well and add to the *dhal* and
mix well. Add the remaining water and salt to taste. Bring to
the boil. Reduce the heat to the lowest setting and cover the
pan. Leave to simmer until both the *dhal* and rice are cooked
and almost all the water absorbed. The rice will not be fluffy as
this dish should have a soft pulpy consistency. Heat the ghee
or oil and brown the finely chopped onions and garlic. Add
this to the *kitchdi* and serve hot.

Kitchdi is made to a pulpy consistency for easy digestion.
Serve with freshly made natural yogurt (page 44).

Spiced Rice with Green Gram
Masala Kitchdi

Serves 4–6

A spiced variation of the previous recipe. Delicious on its own
with yogurt and pickle or with any vegetable curry. For an
alternative method delete the cloves, cinnamon, cardamom
and allspice. This version is what my mother serves with her
'central heating fuel' – Eggs on Garlic Tops (page 144).

2 cups patna rice, picked and
  washed
1 cup green gram (moong
  dhal), picked and washed
4 tablespoons ghee or
  clarified butter
2 heaped tablespoons
  chopped onions
2 cloves garlic, finely crushed
4 thin slices fresh ginger

2 green chillies, left whole
4 cloves
2.5-cm (1-inch) cinnamon
  quill
4 whole cardamoms, bruised
½ teaspoon whole allspice
1 teaspoon turmeric powder
salt to taste
4½ cups hot water

Soak the rice and *dhal* in cold water for about 20 minutes. Melt the ghee or oil in a pan with a tight-fitting lid. Add the onions, garlic, ginger, chillies, cloves, cinnamon, cardamom and allspice and gently fry these until the onions are pale golden. Drain the rice and *dhal* thoroughly and add to the pan. Sauté the rice and *dhal* for 2 or 3 minutes. Add the turmeric powder and salt. Lightly toss the mixture together using a broad, flat, wooden spoon and cook on a very low heat for 5 minutes. Add the water and bring it to the boil. Reduce the heat to the lowest setting and cover the pan. Leave to simmer until the rice and *dhal* are cooked. This will take about 25 minutes. Serve hot, garnished with deep-fried onions and, if you wish, slices of hardboiled egg and tomato.

Note: Although the whole spices are edible, it is advisable to warn your diners that they are in the dish!

Exotic Vegetable Rice
Shahi Deccani Yakhni Pulao

Serves 4–6

It was very lucky that my trip to India in 1984 coincided with the Muslims' great feast of Ramazan (*Id-ul-Fitr*). I was overwhelmed with lunch and dinner invitations and my sister-in-law's family prepared this dish specially for me. They, of course, served it with a number of other dishes but I think it is a complete meal on its own. I know it has a lot of ingredients so leave it in your thoughts and serve it for a special occasion. On its own it will make a hearty meal for 4—6 persons but if you serve it with other dishes it will stretch further.

450g (1 lb) total weight green peas, butter beans, beans, cauliflower and carrots

3 cups basmati rice, picked and washed

6 cups water

350g (12 oz) ghee or white unsalted butter

1 small loaf unsliced bread, cut into small cubes

100g (4 oz) nuts, cashew or almonds or pistachios or mixed

4 green chillies, slit

5 cardamoms, bruised

Ingredients to be ground to a paste (use water to facilitate the grinding)

4 dried chillies

7 cloves garlic

½ teaspoon cumin seeds (or black cumin — shahjeera)

2.5-cm (1-inch) quill cinnamon

3 cloves

2.5-cm (1-inch) piece fresh ginger

½ teaspoon turmeric powder

½ teaspoon grated nutmeg

1 teaspoon salt

Cut all the vegetables into bite-size pieces and blanch them for 1 minute in salted water. Drain and keep aside, reserving the water. In the same water parboil the rice, drain and keep aside. In a wok or a large frying pan, heat the ghee and fry the bread cubes until they are crisp. Drain well and keep aside. Reheat the ghee and fry the nuts, drain and keep aside.

Transfer 6 tablespoons of the ghee to a large heavy pan with a tight-fitting lid. Reheat the ghee and fry the whole chillies and cardamoms. When the chillies start to turn whitish add the ground paste and on a low heat fry until the ghee rises above the masala. Add the vegetables and rice and gently fold them in evenly with the spices. Sprinkle 1 cup of the reserved water over the rice and vegetables and place a round piece of greased foil over it. Cover the pan and on the lowest setting simmer until the rice is fluffy and the vegetables cooked. Garnish with the pieces of fried bread and nuts and serve hot.

Peas and Potato Rice
Mattar Aloo Pilau
Serves 4–6

This rice is prepared all over India. My friend Basil always orders this when he goes to an Indian restaurant. I hope my method will allow him to enjoy this dish at home without having to go to his favourite restaurant which is twenty-nine kilometres away.

2 cups basmati rice, picked and washed
4 teaspoons ghee or oil
6 cloves
½ teaspoon cumin seeds
100g (4 oz) frozen green peas

100g (4 oz) diced potato
2 tablespoons natural yogurt
3½ cups water
salt to taste

Ingredients to be ground to a paste
4 cloves garlic
1.25-cm (½-inch) piece fresh ginger
1 teaspoon garam masala (choose from pages 54–6)

1 medium-sized onion

Soak the rice in cold water for 20 minutes. Heat ghee or oil in a large heavy pan which has a tight-fitting lid. Fry the cloves and cumin seeds until aromatic. Reduce the heat and add the ground paste, peas and potatoes and fry for 5 minutes. Add the yogurt and half a cup of water and allow to simmer until the peas and potatoes are half done. Add the drained rice and stir-fry for 2 minutes. Add the remaining water and salt. Mix well. Bring to the boil over a high heat and when it reaches a boil reduce the heat to the lowest setting, cover the pan and allow to simmer until the rice is fluffy. Serve hot with any vegetable or lentil curry.

Rice with Aubergine
South Indian *Vengi Bhath*
Serves 4—6

In south Indian cooking rice acts as a vehicle for other foods but there are several ways of serving it. This is a simple dish of quickly fried rice and aubergines, making an excellent combination.

3 tablespoons oil
1½ teaspoons mustard seeds
a few curry leaves, chopped
2 dark purple aubergines, cut into bite-size pieces and soaked in cold water
3 green chillies, finely chopped or 1 teaspoon chilli powder

salt to taste
1 teaspoon turmeric powder
4 cups cooked rice, grains loosened
juice of 1 lemon

Heat the oil in a non-stick wok or a large non-stick frying pan and fry the mustard seeds and curry leaves until the mustard

seeds crackle. Drain the aubergines and add with the chillies
to the wok. Stir-fry for a few minutes. Cover the wok or pan
and cook the aubergines for about 10 minutes, stirring
occasionally. If it becomes too dry sprinkle in a few drops of
hot water. Add the salt and turmeric powder and stir well. Add
the rice and with the help of two flat wooden spoons gently
fold it in. Cover the wok or pan again and leave to simmer
until the rice has heated through. Just before serving mix in
the lemon juice. Serve hot with a lentil curry (pages 179–80)
or *rasam* (pages 202–3).

Rice with Aubergine 2
Maharashtran Vangi Bhath
Serves 4–6

The Maharashtrans further complement this dish by adding
nuts, sugar and coconut, and generally serve it with garlic
chutney (*lasun chi chutney*), page 241.

4 tablespoons oil
1 teaspoon mustard seeds
a few curry leaves, chopped
*4 cups patna or basmati rice,
    washed and drained*
*350g (12 oz) dark purple
    aubergine, cut into pieces
    5cm (2 inches) long and
    soaked in water*
6 cups water
*1½ teaspoons coriander
    seeds*
1½ teaspoons cumin seeds
¼ cup desiccated coconut

2 red chillies
*2 teaspoons goda masala
    (page 53)*
*2 teaspoons light brown
    sugar or jaggery*
salt to taste
*15 cashew nuts, deep fried
    and drained*
1 cup natural yogurt, beaten
*1 cup freshly grated coconut
    (optional)*
*fresh coriander leaves for
    garnish*

Heat the oil in a large heavy pan with a tight-fitting lid. Fry the mustard seeds and when they crackle add the curry leaves and drained rice and fry for 2 minutes. Drain the aubergine and add to the rice and mix well. Add the water and bring to the boil. Reduce the heat to the lowest setting, cover the pan and allow to simmer for 5 minutes. In the meantime roast the coriander seeds, cumin seeds, desiccated coconut and chillies and finely grind them in an electric blender. Add to this the *goda masala* and mix well. Add this masala, the sugar, salt and cashew nuts to the rice and mix well. Gradually add the yogurt and gently fold it into the rice. Cover the pan and simmer till the rice is fluffy and loose. Serve hot, garnished with grated coconut and coriander leaves.

Rice Layered with Red Gram
Dhal Chawal

Serves 4–6

I am a Bhori, a small sect of the Shia Muslims. We have our own style of cooking several dishes which is different from other communities in India. Try this rice dish with *palida* (page 190) and *sabzi petis* (page 153).

*1 cup red gram (*tuvar *or* arhar dhal*)*
7 cups water
½ teaspoon turmeric powder
2 cups patna or basmati rice, picked and washed
½ teaspoon salt
2 medium-sized onions, finely sliced and deep fried until crisp (page 58)
4 tablespoons ghee or oil

1 teaspoon cumin powder
1 teaspoon garam masala (pages 54–6)
½ teaspoon chilli powder or 2 green chillies, chopped
4 cloves garlic, crushed
a handful coriander leaves, chopped
a few mint leaves, chopped
½ cup hot water mixed with a little ghee or oil

Cook the *dhal* in 3 cups water and turmeric powder until the grains are cooked but not mushy. Drain the water and keep aside to make the *palida* (page 190). Boil the rice in remaining 4 cups of water and salt until the grains are half cooked. Drain the water and keep the rice aside. In a frying pan heat the ghee or oil and on a medium heat fry the garlic, cumin powder, garam masala, chilli powder, coriander and mint leaves. Fry until the raw smell of the garlic disappears. Gently fold in the cooked *dhal* then remove from the heat. Grease a heavy pan with a tight-fitting lid and put in a layer of rice followed by a layer of *dhal*. Sprinkle some fried onions over the *dhal*. Continue like this, ending with a rice layer. Sprinkle water mixed with ghee or oil all over the rice. Cover the pan and leave to simmer until the rice grains are fluffy. Serve hot.

Tamarind Rice
Puliyodarai
Serves 4—6

In south India tamarind rice is made and offered in temples to the presiding deities and then to the priest and pilgrims. It is usually prepared for mass feeding but I managed to get the recipe from my maid who was one day preparing it for her *puja* — prayers — at a temple.

a fistful of tamarind
½ cup sesame or vegetable oil
¼ teaspoon asafoetida
3 tablespoons bengal gram (channa dhal)
1 teaspoon salt

1 teaspoon turmeric powder
2 teaspoons chilli powder (or reduce to suit)
a few curry leaves
4 cups cooked rice, grains loosened

Soak the tamarind in 1 cup boiling water. Work the tamarind

in the water by squeezing until the water thickens and darkens and the seeds are clean. Pass through a fine sieve and collect the juice. Discard the coarse pulp and seeds. Heat half the oil in a large pan and fry the asafoetida and bengal gram until the gram is a golden colour. Reduce the heat and add the other ingredients except the rice and the remaining oil. Bring to the boil and then simmer until the quantity is reduced by half. Remove from the heat and fold in the rice. Heat the remaining oil and pour over the rice. Mix well and keep covered until ready to serve. If you wish, garnish with fried raw peanuts.

Rice with Gram or Chickpeas
Qubuli
Serves 4–6

This rice dish is usually prepared by the Shia Muslims during the month of Mohurram. This is the first month in the Muslim calendar and also the month when the grandson of Mohammed the Prophet (Peace be on Him) fought the *jehad* — holy war. I learnt this recipe from my brother's wife who is a Deccani Shia Muslim.

1 cup bengal gram (channa dhal) or split chickpeas
4 cups water
2 cups patna or basmati rice, picked and washed
½ teaspoon salt
6 tablespoons ghee or oil
2 medium-sized onions, finely sliced
4 cloves garlic, ground to a paste

5-cm (2-inch) piece fresh ginger, ground to a paste
1 teaspoon cumin seeds
3 cardamoms, bruised
4 green chillies, left whole
10 mint leaves, left whole
½ bunch coriander leaves, coarsely chopped
4 tablespoons yogurt, beaten
salt to taste
4 tablespoons milk

Boil the gram or chickpeas in 2 cups water until soft but not mushy. Drain and set aside, reserving the water. Put the reserved water back in the pan and add the remaining water, rice and salt. Bring to the boil and then simmer uncovered for 5 minutes. Drain the rice and keep aside, loosening the grains gently with a fork to remove the excess steam. Heat the ghee or oil in a frying pan and fry the onions until golden brown. Reduce the heat and add all the spices, herbs and gradually the yogurt. Add salt to taste and mix well. Simmer for 5 minutes or until the sour yogurt smell has disappeared. Add the drained gram and fold in gently to coat the grains evenly with the gravy. Leave aside. Grease the base of a heavy pan with a tight-fitting lid. Place a layer of rice about 2.5cm (1 inch) deep. Put the gram on the rice and make an even layer. Sprinkle a few drops of milk. Cover the gram with the remaining rice. Sprinkle the remaining milk all over the rice. Cover the pan with a sheet of foil and then the lid. Simmer on the lowest heat setting or bake in a moderately hot oven for about 10 minutes. Serve hot.

Rice Layered with Vegetables
Biryani
Serves 4—6

While I was writing this book my mother was visiting me from India. The first time I told her I was cooking *biryani* for about thirty people she thought I was mad. She said it was too much *khit- pit* ('entailed too much work') and was impractical. But I managed to convince her that serving *biryani* as a main course, even for large numbers, is an excellent idea. In India there are rules and regulations for making *biryani* that one has to abide by but I have lived in the UK for over twenty years now and have had to make adjustments to suit my lifestyle here. However, I assure you that the taste of this dish is still authentic.

Rice

4 large onions, finely sliced,
 deep-fried until crisp and
 drained
900g (2 lb) total weight
 cauliflower florets, peas,
 diced carrots
450g (1 lb) small potatoes,
 peeled, deep-fried until
 golden brown and drained
4 cups basmati rice, picked
 and washed

8 cups water
1 teaspoon black cumin seeds
5-cm (2-inch) cinnamon
 quill
1 teaspoon salt
4 fl oz (110 ml) milk
a few strands saffron
4 tablespoons warm milk
6 tablespoons ghee

MARINADE

150g (5 oz) natural yogurt
2 tablespoons tomato purée
1 tablespoon salt
2 tablespoons garam masala

5-cm (2-inch) piece fresh
 ginger, finely crushed
6 cloves garlic, finely crushed
2 tablespoons lemon juice

Crush the deep-fried onions, leaving aside a small quantity for
the garnish. Mix them with all the marinade ingredients and
rub well into the mixed vegetables and fried potatoes. Leave
aside for about 2 hours.

Put the rice, water, cumin seeds, cinnamon and salt in a
large pan and bring to the boil. Lower the heat and simmer
until the rice grains are half cooked. Drain well. Soak the
saffron in the warm milk.

Place the marinated vegetables in a large pan with a tight-
fitting lid. Cover with the half-cooked rice and pour the milk
evenly over the rice. Heat the ghee and pour along the sides of
the pan. Make deep holes with a skewer or the handle of a
wooden spoon and into each hole pour a little of the saffron
mixture. Cover the pan, first with a sheet of foil and then with a
lid. Put on a low heat and let it cook until you hear the ghee
sizzling inside. This will take about 45 minutes. Do not
uncover the pan to check, but sprinkle a little cold water on
the outside of the pan and if it sizzles away very fast your
biryani is done. Serve hot with egg curry (page 217) and a
yogurt salad (pages 208–11).

Dish From Leftover Biryani
Khatyoo
Serves 4—6

If you wish to try this dish prepare extra *biryani* so you are sure to have some left over. It is delicious.

1.2 litres (2 pints) leftover
 biryani

3 cups buttermilk (preferably
 a few days old)

Mix the leftover *biryani* and buttermilk and allow to simmer gently until the buttermilk has been absorbed but is not completely dried out. Serve hot in bowls with spoons. Serve with *kachoomber* (page 252), pickle and *papadums*.

Vegetables

India is a country which provides us with nutritious vegetables, vegetables and more vegetables . . .

The highlight of every city, town or village I visited during my last trip to India was a walk through the vegetable markets. I have travelled round the world but I think India provides us with the greatest wealth of vegetables in the world. For this reason Indian vegetable dishes should rank among the best there are, and they provide the widest range of new ideas which appeal to both vegetarians and non-vegetarians alike.

Vegetable recipes from south India and the states of Gujerat and Maharashtra play a prominent role in this book as south India is mainly vegetarian and the Gujeratis and Maharashtrans are almost entirely vegetarian. I have also included recipes from the other states I visited and several dishes I used to enjoy during the first twenty-one years of my life when I lived with my parents in India.

Several of the vegetables in this chapter are common throughout the world. The unusual ones, which can be found in the UK, are described on pages 15–25 and their popularity is gaining so fast that we should soon be able to find most, if not all, in our supermarkets. Suitable substitutes have been given for the vegetables which are difficult to obtain anywhere other than at an Indian or Chinese grocer.

Finally, here are some golden tips about cooking and eating vegetables.

1. Buy the best, most fresh and tender vegetables you can and cook them as soon as possible.
2. Wash all vegetables under running tap water. This will remove any harmful insecticides and germs.

ible, never peel vegetables or cut them into very
pieces, and do not let them stand for a long time in
water.

4. Boil the water before you add the fresh vegetables, and
   cook them in as little a quantity of water as possible. Do not
   overcook them.
5. Do not add baking soda to retain the natural colour of the
   vegetable as it is harmful to health.
6. Cook the quantity required to avoid having leftovers.
7. Do not eat only one kind of vegetable at a time. Try and
   combine three or four kinds and vary them each day.

Stuffed Okra Fry
Bhara Bhinda Shak
Serves 4–6

This dish comes from the state of Gujerat which is perhaps the
only pure vegetarian state in India. Gujeratis are staunch
vegetarians and they are famous for their protein-packed
snacks and *shaks* – dry vegetable curries.

20 tender okra (lady's fingers
or bhendi)
2 tablespoons desiccated
coconut
½ cup gram flour (besan or
channa atta)
1 teaspoon sugar
1 teaspoon turmeric powder

2 teaspoons chilli powder (or
to taste)
1 teaspoon coriander powder
a pinch asafoetida
2 tablespoons sesame oil
salt to taste
coriander leaves for garnish

Wash and wipe the okra. Cut off the tops sparingly and make a
slit in the centre but not all the way through. Mix together the
coconut, gram flour, sugar, turmeric, chilli powder, coriander
powder, asafoetida and salt with a little water to make a thick

paste. Stuff the okra with the prepared paste. Heat the oil in a large frying pan or a wok. Reduce the heat and add the stuffed okra and fry until they are cooked. Serve hot.

Brussels Sprout Curry
Choti bund Gobhi Khorma
Serves 4–6

I tasted a cabbage *korma* in a small village in India and on my return tried it with Brussels sprouts. It was delicious and even my boys, who usually hate Brussels sprouts, ate it without a battle.

350g (12 oz) Brussels sprouts,	*4 tomatoes, chopped*
fresh or frozen	*1 cup thick coconut milk*
4 tablespoons oil	*(pages 58–60)*
3 onions, finely chopped	*salt to taste*

Ingredients to be dry-roasted and ground

1 teaspoon aniseed (saunf)	*1 cardamom, peeled*
2.5-cm (1-inch) piece fresh	*1 clove*
ginger	*1 bay leaf*
2 cloves garlic	*½ teaspoon cumin seeds*
2.5-cm (1-inch) cinnamon	*a handful coriander leaves*
quill	

Cut a cross on the heads of the Brussels sprouts and keep aside. In a large pan or a wok heat the oil and fry the onions until golden brown in colour. Reduce the heat and add the ground paste and fry until the oil separates. Add the Brussels sprouts and tomatoes and mix well. Add salt to taste and fry for about 5 minutes. Add the coconut milk and bring to the boil. Reduce heat again and cook uncovered until the Brussels sprouts are done and there is a thick gravy. Serve hot with rice or bread.

Mixed Vegetables
Sadi Sabzi
Serves 4–6

My mother regularly made this dish which is delicious as a snack or part of a main meal. It is lightly spiced and very appetizing when served with natural yogurt.

350g (12 oz) mixed frozen vegetables, thawed, or *choose from the following to make up 350g (12 oz): beans, peas, boiled potato cubes, small cauliflower florets, diced carrots, cabbage, mange-touts, tomato, onion, aubergine, turnip and button mushrooms*

2 tablespoons oil
½ teaspoon cumin seeds
¼ teaspoon mustard seeds
6 onion seeds
a pinch turmeric
a few curry leaves
salt to taste
a pinch sugar

If you are using fresh vegetables cut them into bite-size pieces. Keep aside. Heat the oil in a large pan or a wok and fry the cumin seeds, mustard seeds, onion seeds, turmeric powder and curry leaves until the mustard seeds crackle. Add the vegetables and stir-fry for a few minutes. Add salt to taste and sugar. Lower the heat and cover the pan. Simmer until the vegetables are done but do not overcook them and avoid stirring vigorously as this will break up the vegetables. Serve hot and allow each individual to help themselves to natural yogurt to suit their taste.

Cauliflower Roast
Tandoori Phool Gobbi
Serves 4—6

One generally associates *tandoori* dishes with poultry, meat or fish. Vegetables prepared in the same fashion are just as delicious. I have only used cauliflower here but you can also try aubergine, potato, small courgettes, firm tomatoes, onions, and so on. Cut the vegetables in half, then marinate and follow the same procedure as for cauliflower.

1 cauliflower, broken in   *oil for basting*
   large florets

Ingredients to be ground together to a paste

1 onion   *2 ripe tomatoes, skinned*
3 cloves garlic   *110ml (4 fl oz) natural*
2.5-cm (1-inch) piece fresh   *yogurt*
   ginger   *salt to taste*
1 teaspoon chilli powder   *red colouring powder or a*
½ teaspoon turmeric powder   *few drops cochineal*
1 teaspoon coriander powder

Marinate the cauliflower florets in the ground paste for 2—3 hours. Roast on skewers or on a grill tray in a medium hot oven basting occasionally. I like to keep the cauliflower crisp but you can cook it to suit your taste. Serve hot with *pitta* bread or *tandoor roti*, a yogurt salad and chutney.

If you have any left-over, mix with rice and make a *pilau*.

Red Potatoes
Lal Batata
Serves 4–6

This is our favourite dish during the new potato season. It should have a distinctive hot and sour taste, but if you wish to reduce the quantity of chillies add 1 tablespoon of tomato purée with the tamarind juice to obtain the red colour. Choose the very small potatoes, peel them and leave them whole. If you are using large, old potatoes or large new potatoes cut them into bite-size pieces.

450g (1 lb) potatoes
25g (1 oz) whole dry red
  chillies (preferably
  kashmiri)
1½ tablespoons cumin seeds
4 cloves garlic
6 tablespoons oil
4 tablespoons thick tamarind
  juice (page 60)

4 curry leaves
salt to taste
chopped coriander leaves for
  garnish
wedges for lemon or lime for
  garnish

Wash the potatoes and then boil them until three quarters done. When cool enough to handle, peel them and leave them whole if they are small or cut them into cubes. Leave aside.

Soak the chillies in a little warm water until soft. Drain and grind them together with the cumin seeds, and garlic. Heat the oil in a large heavy pan and fry the ground paste until the oil separates. Add the potatoes, tamarind juice, curry leaves and salt to taste. Mix well but gently to prevent the potatoes breaking up. Reduce the heat to the lowest setting, cover the pan and allow to simmer until the raw tamarind juice flavour disappears. Garnish and serve hot. Delicious with *puris*.

Cutlet Express
Cutlet Rail Gadi
Serves 4−6

When I entertain I spend a lot of time preparing the display for each of my dishes. I served this at a children's party and to my amazement they cleaned the plate as quickly as an express train moves.

2 tablespoons oil
1 onion, chopped
225g (8 oz) frozen diced vegetables, thawed and drained
1 teaspoon chopped cashew nuts

½ teaspoon cumin powder
salt and pepper to taste
4 large potatoes, boiled, peeled and mashed
1 egg
breadcrumbs
oil for shallow-frying

To garnish
lettuce leaves
diced carrots for wheels
5-cm (2-inch) piece whole carrot for funnel
round slices cucumber for links

sliced beetroot for engine
boiled peas for track
thin cucumber slices for track

Heat the oil in a large pan and fry the onions until golden brown. Add the frozen vegetables, cashew nuts, cumin powder and salt and pepper to taste. Sauté for a few minutes. Remove from the fire and fold in the mashed potato. Make three square cutlets and the remaining into finger-length round cutlets. Dip them in egg and then cover them with breadcrumbs. Heat oil for shallow-frying and gently fry the cutlets until they are golden brown and crisp. Drain on kitchen paper.

Place the lettuce leaves on a large serving platter. Place the cutlets and garnish to make it look like a train, using the square cutlets for the engine and carriage and finger cutlets for the track.

Drumstick and Potato Curry
Sekta Singh aur Aloo
Serves 4–6

This recipe does not come from any particular state of India —
it was invented in my kitchen in Suffolk.

6 medium thick drumsticks
4 tablespoons oil
1 onion, finely chopped
2 whole dry red chillies
½ teaspoon cumin seeds
6 onion seeds
½ teaspoon turmeric powder
a pinch asafoetida

a few curry leaves
½ teaspoon sugar
salt to taste
2 teaspoons tomato purée
2 potatoes, boiled, peeled and cubed
lemon juice

Scrape the drumsticks and cut them into 5-cm (2-inch) pieces.
Heat oil in a wok or a large frying pan which has a lid. Fry the
onions and spices until the onions are soft and a light golden
colour. Add sugar and salt to taste. Add the drumstick pieces
and mix well. Sprinkle on a little hot water and cover the wok
or frying pan. Cook on a low flame until the drumsticks are
done (about 20–30 minutes). Check occasionally that the
mixture is not too dry as it will burn. (To avoid this you can put
some water on the hollow of the wok lid or cover your frying
pan with a flat lid with some water on it.) When the drumsticks
are cooked fold in the tomato purée and potato. Mix well and
serve hot. Add lemon juice to taste.

The drumsticks are not totally edible even after fully
cooking them. Either hold the pieces in your hand and suck
the pulp or chew the pieces until dry and discard the coarse
peel. Do not be shy of doing this. If you are to begin with, I can
assure you that you will not be once you have tasted this
delicious vegetable.

Sweet Corn Curry
Butte Ka Salan
Serves 4–6

In India the most popular way of eating corn on the cob is roasting it on charcoal, rubbing it with a slice of lemon and sprinkling it with salt and chilli powder. When in season there are hundreds of roadside vendors filling the atmosphere with the delicious aroma of roasted corn. Each state prepares their own versions of corn curry but I think my recipe is a combination of the Maharashtran and south Indian styles.

4 corn cobs, tinned or frozen
oil for frying
½ teaspoon turmeric powder
6 onion seeds (kalonji)
½ teaspoon cumin seeds
a few curry leaves
½ teaspoon five-spice
  powder

chilli powder and salt to taste
½ teaspoon sugar
200ml (7 fl oz) natural
  yogurt, beaten
lemon wedges and chopped
  coriander leaves for
  garnish

Ingredients to be ground to a paste
1 large onion, chopped
2 cloves garlic
6-mm (1-inch) piece fresh ginger

Cut the cobs into three pieces, using a heavy knife or a chopper as this will make clean cuts and avoid damaging the kernels. Heat the oil in a wok or a large pan and fry the cob pieces until golden brown on all sides. Remove and keep aside. Remove any excess oil leaving about 4 tablespoons in the wok or pan. Heat the oil and fry the ground paste until the raw smell disappears. Add the remaining ingredients except the yogurt and cob pieces. Cook for about 2 minutes on a medium heat or until the oil separates. Reduce the heat and lly add the yogurt, mixing well to avoid curdling. Add the cob pieces and cover them with the gravy. Cover the wok or pan and allow to simmer until the corn is cooked and the gravy thick. Serve hot with lemon wedges and chopped coriander leaves. Once again, do not hesitate to use your fingers and, after biting off the kernels, suck the corn as it will have absorbed all the delicious gravy.

This also makes a pleasant starter and your guests can clean their hands before they proceed with the rest of the meal.

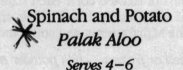

Spinach and Potato
Palak Aloo

Serves 4–6

India is blessed with over eighteen varieties of spinach. If you have access to an Indian or Chinese grocer you will be able to find some of these varieties. Ordinary spinach is widely available but you can substitute carrot leaves, radish leaves and beetroot leaves which are available in the summer months.

4 tablespoons oil
225g (8 oz) potato, peeled, washed and quartered
2.5-cm (1-inch) piece of fresh ginger, finely crushed
4 cloves garlic, finely crushed
2 green chillies, left whole
½ teaspoon chilli powder

225g (8 oz) spinach leaves, coarsely chopped (use frozen spinach if necessary)
salt to taste
a handful fresh coriander leaves, chopped

Heat the oil and fry the potatoes until brown on all sides. Remove and keep aside. Remove excess oil and in the same pan fry the ginger, garlic, chillies and chilli powder. Add the spinach and fry for 1 minute. Add the potatoes and salt to taste.

120

Mix well and cover the pan and cook on a slow fire until the potatoes are done. Sprinkle on a little hot water if necessary. Garnish with coriander leaves and serve hot with any bread preparation or as one of the main course dishes.

Spinach and Vegetable Pie
Bhaji Sabzi Handi
Serves 4—6

Serve this dish hot or cold with a crisp green salad. I also serve slices of this pie with boiled pasta to which I add my favourite fresh herbs — like coriander, mint and dill — and sprinkle some olive mixed with lemon juice, salt and pepper.

15g (½ oz) butter or margarine

100g (4 oz) spring onions, finely chopped

100g (4 oz) onion, finely chopped

4 green chillies, finely chopped (or to taste)

2.5-cm (1-inch) piece fresh ginger, crushed

3 cloves garlic, crushed

a handful fresh coriander leaves, chopped

450g (1 lb) frozen mixed vegetables, thawed and drained

250g (9 oz) frozen chopped spinach, thawed and excess water removed

salt to taste

3 eggs

Heat the butter and sauté spring onions, onion, ginger, garlic, chillies and coriander leaves. Add the mixed vegetables and stir well. Remove from heat and add spinach and mix well. Add salt to taste. Beat the eggs well and add to the vegetables and spinach. Mix well. Pour into a greased pie dish and bake at 180°C (350°F), gas mark 4, for about 30 minutes.

Fenugreek Leaf Balls
Methi Vadai

Serves 4–6 (or more as a cocktail snack)

Fenugreek spinach has a slightly bitter taste yet it is one of our favourite vegetables. You can grow your own by planting fenugreek seeds in shallow trays with loose soil. Fenugreek spinach should be picked when the first two leaves appear.

4 teaspoons oil
4 cloves garlic, crushed
a pinch each clove powder,
  cinnamon powder and
  cardamom powder (or ½
  teaspoon five-spice powder)
250g (9 oz) bengal gram
  (channa dhal) soaked
  overnight
225g (8 oz) fenugreek leaves,
  picked, washed and
  drained
1 bunch dill leaves (suva),
  picked, washed and
  drained

250g (9 oz) ridge gourd
  (turai), peeled, pith
  removed and sliced
250g (9 oz) potatoes, peeled,
  boiled and mashed
1 teaspoon dry mango
  powder (amchur) or a few
  drops of lemon juice
salt to taste
oil for deep-frying

Heat the oil and fry the garlic and powdered spices on a low flame. Add the drained *dhal*, chopped greens, ridge gourd (soak in salt water for 2 hours beforehand if you wish to remove some of the bitter taste) and chillies. Cook on a slow fire until all the ingredients are cooked and the liquid evaporated. Grind to a fine paste. Add the mashed potato, *amchur* and salt. Mix well. Form into small balls and fry in hot oil until evenly brown and crisp. Serve hot with coriander chutney (page 239)

Fenugreek and Potato
Methi Bhaji Aloo
Serves 4−6

Fenugreek and potato complement each other. The bitter taste of fenugreek is softened by the gentle taste of potato. I use new potatoes whenever available and it is worth paying the little extra for them when imported out of season.

5 tablespoons oil
225g (8 oz) onions, finely chopped
½ teaspoon turmeric powder
250g (9 oz) potato, washed, peeled, quartered and placed in cold water
225g (8 oz) fenugreek leaves, picked, washed and drained

100g (4 oz) tomatoes, chopped
4 cloves garlic, crushed
salt to taste
200ml (7 fl oz) natural yogurt, beaten

Heat the oil and brown the onion slightly. Add the turmeric and drained potatoes and continue frying for a few minutes. Cover the pan and allow to simmer until the potatoes are nearly done. Add a few drops of hot water if necessary. Add the remaining ingredients except the yogurt and mix well. Remove the pan from the heat and after about 5 minutes fold in the yogurt gradually. Mix well and adjust salt to taste. Before serving reheat over a low flame to avoid curdling.

Simple Spinach
Palak Sag 1
Serves 4–6

This is the way my Sindhi friends prepare spinach, delicious when served with *puris*, natural yogurt and pickles. It may seem a lot of spinach but remember it gets cooked down to less than half its original quantity.

900g (2lb) spinach, picked, washed and drained
1 heaped teaspoon chilli powder
2.5-cm (1-inch) piece fresh ginger, crushed

50g (2 oz) ghee or unsalted butter
50g (2 oz) onion, finely chopped
salt to taste

Coarsely chop the spinach. Cook in a heavy pan with 1 cup water, chilli powder and ginger. Cover the pan and cook until the spinach is done. Mash well with a potato masher. In a small frying pan heat the ghee or butter and fry the chopped onion until brown. Add the ghee and onion to the spinach and mix well. Add salt to taste and serve hot.

You can use 225g (8 oz) frozen chopped spinach if you wish. Thaw the spinach completely and drain off some of the excess juice.

Simple Spinach
Palak Sag 2
Serves 4—6

See how each community makes their own variation. The previous recipe was Sindhi style but this is the way spinach is prepared in my home. I serve it hot with chappatis.

4 tablespoons oil
2 whole dry chillies, seeded
  for a milder flavour
4 cloves garlic, thinly sliced
1 heaped teaspoon cumin
  powder

2 large onions, coarsely
  sliced
900g (2 lb) spinach, picked,
  washed and drained then
  chopped coarsely
salt to taste

Heat the oil and when hot reduce the heat and fry the red chillies until they are dark brown in colour. Lower the heat further if possible and add the garlic, cumin powder and onions. Continue frying until the onions are soft. Coarsely chop the spinach, add to the pan and salt to taste. Mix well. Cover the pan and allow to simmer for a few minutes. Do not overcook the spinach — the colour should remain as green as possible. Serve hot, and garnish with chopped tomatoes if you wish.

Spinach Cutlet
Palak Kebabs

Serves 4–6 (or more as a starter or snack)

These are delicious when accompanied with a lentil curry and
pilau rice. They can also be served as a snack or cocktail bites.
The green chillies are very prominent in this dish but you can
adjust the quantity to suit your taste.

250g (9 oz) bengal gram
(channa dhal), *washed and
drained*
900g (2 lb) spinach, picked,
*washed, drained and chop-
ped coarsely, or 225g (8 oz)
frozen chopped spinach*
2 teaspoons oil
75g (3 oz) onion, finely
chopped
2.5-cm (1-inch) piece fresh
ginger, finely crushed

4 cloves garlic, finely crushed
4 green chillies, finely
chopped
1 teaspoon garam masala
salt to taste
a handful fresh coriander
leaves, finely chopped
1 egg white
150g (5 oz) white
breadcrumbs
oil for deep-frying

Boil the *dhal* in 3 cups water and then simmer until tender.
Add the spinach and cook until all the water has evaporated. (If
you are using frozen spinach allow most of the water to
evaporate before adding to the *dhal*.) Mash the *dhal* and
spinach to a thick paste with a potato masher. Heat the oil in a
separate pan and fry the onions, ginger, garlic, green chillies
and garam masala. Add the mixture of *dhal* and spinach and
salt to taste. Cook for a few minutes. Cool the mixture and add
the chopped coriander leaves. Make cutlets and dip each in
beaten egg white and then roll in breadcrumbs. Deep-fry in
hot oil until brown and crisp.

Fenugreek Spinach and Egg
Methi-Anda Bhaji
Serves 4—6

A simple Parsi-style dish. This can also be served as a cocktail snack on small pieces of French toast.

225g (8 oz) fenugreek leaves, picked, washed and drained well
2 tablespoons ghee or oil
2 large onions, finely chopped

4 green chillies, finely chopped
1 teaspoon ginger paste
salt and pepper to taste
6 eggs, beaten

Chop the fenugreek leaves. Heat the ghee or butter and lightly fry the onions. Add the spinach, chillies, ginger, salt and pepper. Mix well and keep frying until the spinach is almost cooked. Add the beaten eggs and fry well until set like scrambled eggs. Serve hot with chappatis or on freshly made toast.

Onions and Cabbage
Piyaz Gobhi
Serves 4−6

A delicious dish made from two of our most common vegetables. Serve as part of a main course or top it with beaten natural yogurt and serve as a starter.

2 tablespoons oil
½ teaspoon cumin seeds
2.5-cm (1-inch) cinnamon
  quill
2 green chillies, finely
  chopped

2 large onions, finely sliced
200g (7 oz) cabbage,
  shredded
¼ teaspoon turmeric powder
salt to taste

Heat the oil in a large pan and fry the cumin seeds until aromatic. Reduce the heat and add cinnamon, green chillies and onions. Fry until the onions are golden brown. Then add the cabbage, turmeric powder and salt. Cover the pan and cook on a slow fire until the cabbage is done. (I undercook the cabbage as I like the crunchy texture.) Garnish with coriander leaves and sprinkle a little lemon juice if desired.

Mushrooms and Peas
Guchi Mattar
Serves 4–6

Fresh mushrooms are not widely available in India except in certain states, therefore the tinned variety are mostly used.

4 tablespoons oil
1 medium-sized onion, finely
  chopped
225g (8 oz) tiny button
  mushrooms, washed and
  left whole

1 cup peas
1 cup natural yogurt, a few
  days old
salt to taste

Ingredients to be ground together
1 onion
a few mint leaves
a few coriander leaves
3 green chillies
3 cloves garlic
2.5-cm (1-inch) piece fresh
  ginger
1 teaspoon poppy seeds, dry-
  roasted

½ tablespoon turmeric
  powder
1 teaspoon chilli powder
  (optional)
1 teaspoon garam masala or
  five-spice powder

To garnish
chopped or quartered
  tomatoes

coriander leaves, chopped

Heat the oil and fry the chopped onion and the ground paste until the raw smell disappears and the oil separates. Add the mushrooms, peas, salt to taste and a little water. Gradually add the yogurt and stir well. Continue cooking over a slow heat until the gravy thickens and the mushrooms and peas are cooked. Garnish and serve hot.

Cabbage Cutlets
Bund Gobhi Kebabs
Serves 4—6

In this recipe the cabbage has to be boiled in salted water. I reserve the water for cooking the rice or lentils which will accompany this dish. The water can also be had as a light soup garnished with coriander leaves, lemon juice and pepper to taste.

*1 large cabbage, washed and
  leaves left whole*
4 eggs
1 cup rice flour
salt to taste
a pinch chilli powder
*3 green chillies, finely
  chopped*

*a little fresh coriander leaves,
  finely chopped*
breadcrumbs for coating
oil for deep-frying
*coriander leaves and tomato
  slices, to garnish*

Boil the cabbage leaves in salted water until well cooked. Drain the water and place the leaves on a plate in a pile. Place another plate over it and squeeze out as much of the water as possible. Repeat several times until the cabbage leaves have flattened in between the plates. Make a batter with the eggs, rice flour, salt, chilli powder, green chillies and coriander leaves. Cut the cabbage leaves into small pieces and roll them carefully in the batter and then in the breadcrumbs. Fry each piece until golden brown on both sides. Garnish with coriander leaves and tomato slices. Serve hot.
Note: Keep a bowl of warm water nearby to clean your hands regularly while using the batter and breadcrumbs.

Tomato Juice Curry
Tamatar Cut
Serves 4–6

This is traditionally a hot curry popular in the Deccan region. I have only used fresh chillies but if you enjoy a hotter dish add ½-1 teaspoon chilli powder when adding the other powdered spices.

½ pint (300ml) tomato juice
*1 tablespoon bengal gram flour (*besan *or* channa atta*)*
salt to taste
1 tablespoon coriander powder
1 teaspoon turmeric powder

4 tablespoons oil
4 green chillies, slit on one side
1 teaspoon cumin seeds
1 teaspoon fenugreek seeds
a few curry leaves
a handful fresh coriander leaves, chopped
juice of 1 lemon

Mix the tomato juice and flour until smooth. Place in a heavy pan and add salt to taste, coriander and turmeric powder. Mix well and simmer. While the curry is simmering heat the oil in a frying pan and when hot reduce the heat and fry the green chillies, cumin seeds, fenugreek seeds and curry leaves. When aromatic pour the oil and spices over the curry and cover the pan immediately. Just before serving reheat well and garnish with coriander leaves and lemon juice. Serve with *pilau* rice or *biryani* (page 108). To make it more elegant float halved hardboiled eggs on the surface of the gravy.

Tomato and Coconut Curry
Tamatar Aur Nariyal Sherwa
Serves 4—6

Serve this curry with *pilau* and several other dry dishes. Serve freshly toasted or fried *papadums* as an accompaniment.

900g (2 lbs) very ripe red tomatoes
1 cup thick coconut milk (page 59)
1 cup thin coconut milk (page 59)
3 green chillies, left whole
2.5-cm (1-inch) piece fresh ginger, crushed

4 onions, sliced
1 clove garlic, crushed
a few coriander leaves, chopped
2 tablespoons ghee
salt to taste
2 tablespoons oil
1 teaspoon mustard seeds

Ingredients to be ground together
6 dried red chillies, seeded for a milder flavour
1 teaspoon cumin seeds

2.5-cm (1-inch) piece fresh ginger
1 tablespoon coriander seeds

Wash the tomatoes and put them in boiling water for a few minutes, then peel and mash them to a purée. Heat the ghee in a large pan and mix all the ingredients except the mustard seeds and oil. Bring to the boil. Reduce the heat and allow to simmer for 30 minutes or until there is a nice thick gravy. Heat the oil in a small frying pan and when nearly smoking add the mustard seeds and fry until they crackle. Pour the oil and mustard seeds over the tomato curry and cover the pan immediately. Serve hot.

Bitter Gourd with Bengal Gram
Karela aur Channa Dhal
Serves 4—6

When my mother-in-law was visiting us from Malaysia I had to include bitter gourd in her diet as she suffered from diabetes — and it is an established fact that this vegetable greatly helps those with this illness. This is a very common dish but my recipe has a distinctive Gujerati and Muslim flavour.

*225g (8 oz) bitter gourd
(karela)*
salt
*50g (2 oz) bengal gram
(channa dhal), picked and
washed*
*oil for deep-frying and a little
ghee or unsalted butter*
1 teaspoon turmeric powder
*2.5-cm (1-inch) piece fresh
ginger, crushed*

1 teaspoon chilli powder
1 teaspoon coriander powder
2 green chillies, chopped
juice of 1 lemon
*a handful fresh coriander
leaves, chopped*
a pinch garam masala
1 teaspoon cumin seeds

Scrape the skin off the *karelas* and cut them into small pieces. Remove the pith and seeds and rub them generously with salt and leave aside for 2 hours. Drain off the excess juice and wash off the salt under running water three or four times. Place the *karelas* in salted water and cook until they are half done. Drain well and dry. Heat enough oil for deep-frying and when smoking hot fry the *karelas* until light brown. Remove and keep aside. In a separate pan cook the *dhal* in 1 cup water, adding salt, turmeric powder, sliced ginger, chilli powder, coriander powder and green chillies. When *dhal* is tender but not mushy add the *karelas* and cook together until the *karelas* are fully done. Add lemon juice, chopped coriander leaves and garam masala. Continue cooking for a few more minutes. Just before serving heat a little ghee and when hot fry the cumin seeds. When the cumin seeds have turned a dark brown colour pour over the *karelas* and mix well. Serve hot.

Spiced Bitter Gourd
Masala Karelas
Serves 4—6

The bitterness of this vegetable provides an interesting taste when cooked with sweet and sour agents like tamarind and jaggery.

4 medium-sized bitter gourd
4 tablespoons oil
1 teaspoon cumin seeds
2 large onions, chopped
2 green chillies, chopped
2 cloves garlic, crushed
a handful of fresh coriander leaves, chopped
¼ teaspoon garam masala (pages 54—6)

1 teaspoon chilli powder or to taste
salt to taste
4 tablespoons tamarind juice (page 60)
4 tablespoons jaggery or brown sugar
1 large tomato, chopped

Scrape, wash and slice the bitter gourd, discarding the pith and seeds. Soak them in cold salted water for 1—2 hours. Heat the oil in a large pan and fry the cumin seeds until aromatic. Add the onions and fry until they are pale yellow in colour. Drain the bitter gourd and add to the pan. Sauté well. Reduce the heat and add the chillies, garlic, half the coriander leaves and powdered spices. Sprinkle a little water and add salt to taste. Cover the pan and cook until the bitter gourd is nearly done. Add the tamarind juice and jaggery. Allow to simmer until the jaggery has dissolved and the oil rises to the surface. Garnish with the remaining coriander leaves and tomato and serve hot with chappatis. If you find the bitter taste too distinctive sprinkle on some lemon juice.

Mixed Vegetables in Coconut and Yogurt
Aviyal
Serves 4—6

Aviyal is the Malabar masterpiece. It is prepared in many of the celebrated south Indian temples for mass feedings and brass vessels three metres in diameter and 1.5 metres deep are often used. The vegetables traditionally used are gourds, raw banana, yam, aubergine, beans, raw mango, drumsticks, cucumber, potato, carrots, peas and pumpkin. Use whatever is available, in proportions according to your choice.

¼ pint (150ml) water
450g (1 lb) mixed vegetables
prepared and cut into bite-size pieces
½ green mango, sliced (optional)

150ml (5 fl oz) natural yogurt, a few days old
3—4 curry leaves

Ingredients to be ground together
4 tablespoons desiccated coconut
2 cloves garlic
3 fresh green chillies, seeded for a milder flavour

1 teaspoon cumin seeds
1 teaspoon salt

Bring the water to the boil in a large pan and simmer the vegetables until half done. Reduce the heat and add the coconut mixture, mango, yogurt and curry leaves, and continue to simmer until the vegetables are fully cooked. Serve hot.

In India just before removing from the heat, 5 tablespoons of raw coconut oil are added just to enhance the flavour further. If it is readily available do try it.

Saffron Pumpkin
Lal Kaddu
Serves 4—6

When cooked this dish glows with the colour of saffron. Blending in the fennel seeds and coconut milk makes it very delicious.

450g (1 lb) pumpkin, peeled, and seeds removed
salt
4 tablespoons oil
1 large onion, finely chopped
2.5-cm (1-inch) piece fresh ginger, finely crushed
1 clove garlic, finely crushed
1/2 teaspoon fennel seeds

3—4 curry leaves
2 fresh red chillies, seeded and coarsely chopped
1 1/2 teaspoons mustard seeds
1 teaspoon turmeric powder
110ml (4 fl oz) thick coconut milk (pages 58—60)
a few chopped coriander leaves to garnish

Cut the pumpkin into cubes and sprinkle with a little salt. Heat the oil in a large heavy pan and fry the onion, ginger, garlic, fennel seeds, curry leaves and chopped chillies until the onions are soft. Stir in the pumpkin, mustard seeds and turmeric. Fry for 1—2 minutes, then reduce the heat and pour in the coconut milk. Cook uncovered for 7—10 minutes, or until the pumpkin is tender and a little mushy. Add salt to taste. Serve hot, garnished with coriander leaves. This curry is delicious with hot chappatis or *puris*.

Tender Bamboo Shoot Curry
Bansa Sag
Serves 4—6

Bamboo shoots are mainly used by the Coorg and Manglorian Christians. The Coorgi people use a lot of bamboo sticks. Split bamboo sticks or *bothu*, as they are called, are used during the Cauvery Festival, during which bamboo receptacles are used to carry the holy spring water from the little *kunike* where the Cauvery river emerges. Before the festivities commence the housewife fetches the holy water which she will use for the day's cooking. During this festival the Coorgs remain pure vegetarians.

*1 large tin bamboo shoots
in brine, drained*
¼ teaspoon turmeric powder
1 teaspoon chilli powder
salt to taste
½ fresh coconut, grated
2 onions
6 cloves garlic

2 teaspoons cumin powder
2 tablespoons rice flour
a pinch mustard
½ teaspoon pepper
4 tablespoons oil
a few curry leaves
1 teaspoon mustard seeds

Mix bamboo shoots (sliced if necessary), chilli powder and salt. Leave aside. Grind the coconut, onions and clove to a paste and add to the bamboo shoots. Mix the cumin powder, rice flour, mustard and pepper with a little water to a smooth paste. Add to the bamboo shoots. Place the pan on a medium heat and gently cook for about 15 minutes, stirring occasionally. Heat the oil in a frying pan and when smoking hot add the curry leaves and mustard seeds. Fry until the mustard seeds crackle and then immediately pour over the bamboo shoots and cover the pan. Serve hot with *bhaturas* (page 237).

Drumstick Curry (Parsi Style)
Sekta Doroo
Serves 4—6

Chew each piece of drumstick (moringa fruit) until all the pulp has been extracted and then discard the coarse string-like peel. You may wish to eat this vegetable delicately by sliding each piece between the front teeth to obtain the pulp but the real fun is in chewing them. Try it and don't be shy.

1 teaspoon coriander seeds
1 teaspoon cumin seeds
6 cloves garlic
2.5-cm (1-inch) piece fresh ginger
2 tablespoons desiccated coconut
14 medium-sized drumsticks (sekta), scraped, washed and cut into 5-cm (2-inch) pieces

2 tablespoons ghee or oil
1 onion, finely chopped
2 cups thick coconut milk (pages 58–60)
1 dessertspoon jaggery or brown sugar
1 teaspoon turmeric powder
½ cup tamarind juice (page 60)
salt to taste

Dry-roast coriander seeds, cumin seeds, garlic, ginger and coconut and then grind them to a fine paste. Boil the drumsticks in salted water until tender. Heat the ghee in a pan and fry the onions until golden. Add the ground paste and fry on a low heat for about 5 minutes. Stir in the coconut milk, jaggery, turmeric powder, tamarind and salt to taste. Bring it to the boil. Reduce heat again and allow gravy to simmer for 10—15 minutes. Add the drained drumsticks and mix well. Serve hot.

Vegetable Curry
Kootu
Serves 4—6

A very popular south Indian curry. If you do not wish to use yam or pumpkin try it with turnips, swedes, courgettes, marrow or carrots. You can also use red gram or green gram or 25g (1 oz) of each.

50g (2 oz) bengal gram (channa dhal), picked and washed
100g (4 oz) yam (suran)
100g (4 oz) ashgourd (petha) or pumpkin
1 teaspoon pepper
salt to taste

½ teaspoon turmeric powder
½ fresh coconut, grated or 6 tablespoons desiccated coconut
5 dried red chillies, seeded for a milder flavour
a small piece jaggery or 2 teaspoons brown sugar

Ingredients for final fry (*tarka*) (page 49)

½ fresh coconut, grated or 6 tablespoons desiccated coconut
1 teaspoon mustard seeds
6 tablespoons oil

a few curry leaves
½ teaspoon bengal gram (channa dhal) — optional
a small piece jaggery or 2 teaspoons brown sugar

Cook the *dhal* in three times its volume of water until it is tender but not mushy. Peel and cut the yam and ashgourd to bite size pieces. Add the vegetables, pepper, salt and turmeric to the *dhal* and cook until the vegetables are done. Add a little water if necessary. Meanwhile grind the coconut and chillies to a fine paste and add to the *dhal* and vegetables. Bring to the boil and remove. In a small frying pan heat the oil and fry the grated coconut, mustard seeds, curry leaves and bengal gram until the coconut is a golden colour. Add to the curry together with the jaggery and mix well. Keep covered for a few minutes to allow the jaggery to dissolve. Serve hot with rice or *puris*.

Radish Cutlets
Mooli ke Kebab

Serves 4–6 (or more as a snack)

I learnt this dish from my mother-in-law. I have changed her recipe to kebabs but if you wish leave the *mooli* grated and cook with the ground ingredients until tender and the oil has separated. You can also try the same recipe with grated cucumber but reduce the cooking time.

450g (1 lb) white radish (mooli)
salt
50g (2 oz) onion, finely sliced, deep-fried, drained and crushed
50g (2 oz) gram flour (besan or channa atta)
1 tablespoon desiccated coconut
1 teaspoon poppy seeds, dry-roasted
1 teaspoon five-spice powder
¼ teaspoon mace (javithri) – crushed or powdered
chilli powder to taste
1 small carton natural yogurt
breadcrumbs for coating
oil for shallow-frying
lemon wedges, to garnish

Skin the radish like a carrot and grate (reserve the leaves if you have them and use as a substitute in any spinach recipe). Boil the radish in a little salted water until soft. Drain any excess water and mash the radish lightly. Grind the remaining ingredients with a little yogurt to make a smooth paste. Mix the paste and radish and check seasoning. Add the onion and mix well. Make small kebabs (cutlets) and roll them in breadcrumbs. Heat oil in a large frying pan and shallow-fry a few kebabs at a time until they are evenly brown on both sides. Serve hot with lemon wedges.

Fried Okra
Bhendi Shak
Serves 4—6

This is a very common recipe. You can also try it with *tindla* (gentlemen's toes), small cauliflower florets, sliced aubergines and small cubes of boiled potatoes.

350g (12 oz) okra, washed and dried thoroughly
½ teaspoon turmeric powder
1 teaspoon chilli powder
salt to taste

5 tablespoons oil
½ teaspoon mustard seeds
coriander leaves and tomatoes, to garnish

Cut the okra into 2.5-cm (1-inch) pieces diagonally or very thin round slices to look like stars. Rub them with turmeric powder, chilli powder and salt. Heat the oil in a large frying pan or a wok and fry the mustard seeds until they crackle. Add the okra and fry them uncovered until they are cooked and nearly crisp. Okra has a sticky mucilage and should therefore be fried as quickly as possible. Serve hot garnished with coriander leaves and chopped tomatoes. Delicious when served with yogurt curry (page 206) and *kitchdi* (page 99).

Cauliflower in Tomatoes
Tamatar me Phool Gobhi
Serves 4—6

Cauliflower itself is a highly desired vegetable and when it is cooked in tomato pulp it is wonderful. Save the cauliflower leaves to use in the recipe on page 211.

3 tablespoons oil
a pinch asafoetida
1 cauliflower, cut into small
   florets
5-cm (2-inch) piece fresh
   ginger, finely chopped
salt to taste
½ teaspoon sugar

½ teaspoon turmeric powder
1 teaspoon chilli powder
3 large ripe tomatoes,
   skinned and mashed, or 3
   tablespoons tomato purée
a handful fresh coriander
   leaves, to garnish

Heat the oil in a large pan or wok and when it begins to smoke add the asafoetida and cauliflower and stir-fry for 2 minutes. Reduce the heat and add ginger, salt and sugar and mix well. Cover the pan and allow the cauliflower to cook for about 5 minutes. Move the cauliflower to the sides of the pan and add the turmeric powder, and chilli powder and stir well. Add the tomatoes or purée and mix well. Continue cooking for a few more minutes. Try and keep the cauliflower crisp. Serve hot garnished with coriander leaves.

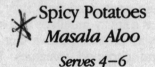

Spicy Potatoes
Masala Aloo

Serves 4–6

This dish should be dry so I recommend that you use a large non-stick frying pan or a wok.

2 tablespoons mustard oil (or
   increase vegetable oil to 5
   tablespoons)
3 cloves
1 teaspoon chilli powder
½ teaspoon cumin powder
1 teaspoon coriander powder
½ teaspoon ginger paste
   (page 56)

½ teaspoon turmeric powder
salt to taste
3 tablespoons vegetable oil
350g (12 oz) small potatoes,
   boiled and thickly sliced
   (peel them if you wish)
a handful fresh coriander
   leaves and lemon wedges,
   to garnish

Heat the mustard oil in a large frying pan or a wok and fry the cloves till they swell. Mix the powdered spices and salt in a little water and keep aside. Add the remaining oil to the pan and then the mixed paste. Stir well and fry on a medium heat until the oil separates from the spices. Stir in the potatoes and stir-fry using a flat spatula to avoid them breaking up. Serve hot garnished with coriander leaves and lemon wedges.

Ginger Curry
Adrak Salan

Serves 4–6 (or more as a pickle)

This is more like a pickle and if you increase the oil it will keep for quite a while in your refrigerator. Always delicious with any lentil dish.

5 tablespoons oil
1 tablespoon grated fresh coconut or desiccated coconut
2 green chillies, chopped
4 tablespoons thick tamarind juice (page 60)

salt to taste
4 heaped tablespoons chopped or grated fresh ginger

Ingredients to be dry-roasted and ground to a paste
20 large dried red chillies
½ teaspoon cumin seeds

½ teaspoon fenugreek seeds
4 cloves garlic

Heat the oil in a heavy pan and fry the coconut until it is a light brown colour. Add the green chillies and the ground masala paste. Fry until you get a fragrant aroma and the oil separates. Pour in the tamarind juice a little at a time and add salt to taste.

Add the ginger and cover and let the gravy simmer until thick.
Serve hot or cool and store.

Garlic Tops with Eggs
Lasan

Serves 4–6

For most of the time in India we are concentrating on how to
keep ourselves cool and give no thought to the few months
when the temperature does fall. This dish is my mother's
answer to central heating. She serves it during the month of
November and promises we shall be warm till February. Serve
it in the UK in May or early June when the garlic tops are
beginning to appear in gardens or pots.

*18 tender garlic tops, finely
 chopped*
1 or 2 eggs per person

*350g (12 oz) ghee or
 unsalted butter*

Place the chopped garlic tops in a hot ovenproof dish. Gently
break the eggs over the garlic. Heat the ghee or butter until
nearly boiling. Pour the ghee or butter over the eggs and leave
until the whites of the eggs begin to set. Serve hot. My mother
uses a metal plate which is placed over a hollow brass ring in
which embers are placed so the ghee is constantly hot. She
serves this dish with rice and green gram (*kitchdi*). Do not
drink any water or cold fluids for a while after you have eaten
this dish in order for it to be effective. The garlic aroma and
taste are very distinctive and if you wish to freshen your mouth
have a cup of hot spiced tea or coffee.

Corn Cutlets
Butta Kebabs
Serves 4–6

Serve these as cutlets along with other dishes or add them to the yogurt curry instead of the plain fritters (page 206). If you are serving them with the curry, make some *kitchdi* (page 99) as well.

225g (8 oz) tinned corn kernels, drained well
150g (5 oz) potatoes, peeled, boiled and mashed
100g (4 oz) gram flour (besan or channa atta)
3 tablespoons natural yogurt
a pinch cooking soda
1 green chilli, very finely chopped

½ teaspoon each cumin powder, garam masala, chilli powder and turmeric powder
a few coriander leaves, finely chopped
salt to taste
oil for deep-frying

Grind the corn coarsely and mix with the remaining ingredients except the oil to make a batter. Mix well until the batter is light and fluffy. Heat the oil in a deep frying pan and when hot drop spoonfuls of the batter and fry until evenly brown. Fry one less than the number of kebabs your pan can accommodate to enable you to turn them over. Serve hot with a chutney of your choice.

145

Stuffed Aubergines
Bhare Huvey Baingan
Serves 4—6

This dish makes a complete meal when served with a pasta and vegetable salad.

4 medium-sized, dark purple
   aubergines
1 large onion, finely chopped
1 cup cooked rice
1 tablespoon tomato purée
1 sweet potato, peeled, boiled
   and cubed

2 green chillies, finely
   chopped
a handful coriander leaves,
   chopped
salt to taste
6 tablespoons oil

Ingredients to be ground together
½ teaspoon turmeric powder   6 cloves garlic
2 dried whole red chillies

Bake the aubergines in a hot oven for about 5 minutes. Cut each aubergine at the tail end and gently scoop out the pulp without damaging the peels. Save the tips to reseal the aubergines. Heat 2 tablespoons oil in a large heavy frying pan and fry the ground ingredients for about 2 or 3 minutes. Add the chopped onions and green chillies and fry until the onions are soft. Lower the heat and fold in the rice, sweet potatoes, tomato purée and aubergine pulp. Remove from the fire and divide the mixture and fill the hollow aubergine peels. Replace the tips and secure with toothpicks. Heat the remaining oil in a large frying pan and add the prepared aubergines. Lower the heat and cover the pan. Cook for about 5 minutes turning the aubergines once carefully. Serve hot.

Stuffed Potatoes
Bhare Huvey Aloo
Serves 4

This dish comes from the states of Gujerat and Maharashtra. Why not try it when you feel like having jacket potatoes? Use large new potatoes whenever possible.

4 large potatoes
1 medium-sized onion, chopped
½ cup small frozen peas
a few coriander leaves, chopped
½ cup desiccated coconut

½ teaspoon garam masala
1 large tomato, skinned and chopped
1½ cups tepid water
6 tablespoons oil
salt to taste

Ingredients to be ground together

1 medium-sized onion
4 cloves garlic
2.5-cm (1-inch) piece fresh ginger
a few coriander leaves

1 green chilli
¼ teaspoon chilli powder
2 teaspoons curry powder (page 52)

Wash the potatoes well and cut off a thin slice lengthwise. Save the slices in water to recap stuffed potatoes. With a small sharp knife scoop out a hollow in the potatoes. Also put these potatoes in water to avoid discoloration. Cut the scooped-out bits into small cubes and soak in water separately. Heat 2 tablespoons oil and fry the chopped onions on a low heat until golden brown. Add the peas, potato bits, corriander leaves, coconut and garam masala. Cover the pan and cook the peas and potatoes. Remove from the heat. Drain the hollowed potatoes well and fill each with equal amounts of the pea mixture. Replace the potato slices and secure with toothpicks. Heat the remaining oil in a large pan or wok and fry the

147

nd ingredients until the raw smell disappears and the oil separates from the spices. Add the tomato and water and bring to the boil. Reduce the heat, carefully put the stuffed potatoes into the pan and cover. Cook until the potatoes are done. Serve hot.

Potato and Onions
Aloo Piyaz
Serves 4–6

This is a very simple way of preparing potatoes but it is a wholesome dish and ideal for hungry children when they get home from school.

2 tablespoons ghee or oil
2 onions, finely chopped
1 teaspoon cumin powder

4 large potatoes, peeled,
*   boiled and cut into chips*
salt to taste

Heat the ghee and fry the onions and cumin powder until the onions are golden brown. Add the potato and salt. Stir well, remove from the heat and serve hot on toast with tomato ketchup.

Potato Cutlets
Aloo Tikkis

Serves 4–6 (or more as a snack)

My cousin Zeenat taught me how to make this dish. Serve with
Dal Chawal (page 105) and Palida (page 190).

4 slices white bread
450g (1 lb) potatoes, boiled,
  peeled and mashed
1 teaspoon cumin powder
10 peppercorns, ground
salt to taste
1 teaspoon dry mango
  powder (amchur) *or juice*
  of 1 lemon
a few coriander leaves, finely
  chopped

4 green chillies, finely
  chopped
2 tablespoons oil
1 large onion, finely chopped
100g (4 oz) small frozen peas
1 teaspoon garam masala
  (pages 54–6)
ghee for shallow-frying

Soak the bread in water for a few minutes, remove and
squeeze them. Mash the bread and mix with the mashed
potatoes, cumin powder, peppercorns, salt, *amchur*,
coriander leaves and green chillies. Knead well and keep
aside. Heat the oil and fry the onion and peas until the onion
turns lightly brown. Add the garam masala and salt to taste.
Take a portion of the mashed potato and make a flat cutlet on
your palm. Place a little pea mixture and roll into a croquette.
When you have prepared all the croquettes heat some ghee for
shallow-frying and fry the croquettes on a low fire until lightly
browned on all sides. Serve hot with a chutney of your choice.

Coconut and Yogurt Curry
Nariyal Dahi Shak
Serves 4—6

This is a Gujerati variation of the popular south Indian *aviyal* (page 135).

1 white radish or turnip,
peeled and sliced
lengthways
2 corn on the cob, each cut
into 3 pieces
2 drumsticks, scraped and cut
into 5-cm (2-inch) pieces
salt
1 cup natural yogurt (a few
days old)
2 tablespoons gram flour
(besan or channa atta)

2 tablespoons oil
a pinch asafoetida
¼ teaspoon turmeric powder
2.5-cm (1-inch) piece fresh
ginger, crushed
1 dried red chilli
a few curry leaves
1 cup thick coconut milk
(pages 58–60)
mint or coriander leaves and
deep-fried onion slices, to
garnish

Blanch all the vegetables separately in salted boiling water for 1 minute. Drain and keep aside, reserving the water. Mix the yogurt, gram flour and 2 cups of the reserved water. Beat with an electric hand whisk until there are no lumps. Pour the yogurt mixture into a large heavy pan and allow to simmer. In a separate frying pan or a wok heat the oil and on a low heat fry the asafoetida, turmeric powder, ginger, red chilli and curry leaves. When the raw smell of the ginger disappears add the blanched vegetables and sauté them for a few minutes. Add the vegetables and spices to the yogurt mixture and continue to simmer until the vegetables are nearly done. Add the coconut milk and leaving the pan uncovered bring to a quick boil. Adjust salt if necessary. Serve hot, garnished with mint or coriander leaves and deep-fried onion slices (page 58).

Stuffed Green Tomatoes
Bhare Huvy Hare Tamatar
Serves 4–6

My dear friend Nini, who is a Gujerati but married to a Muslim, gave me this delicious recipe when I visited her in Poona. She has learnt to prepare Muslim dishes for her husband but still retains her distinctive Gujerati upbringing.

6 large green tomatoes
6 tablespoons desiccated
  coconut
½ teaspoon coriander
  powder
½ teaspoon cumin powder
¼ teaspoon turmeric powder

¼ teaspoon chilli powder
1 clove garlic, crushed
1 teaspoon sugar
salt to taste
2 tablespoons oil
a pinch asafoetida

Make deep crosses in the tomatoes but do not cut them all the way through. Gently ease the quarters to form a little hollow. Mix together the remaining ingredients except the oil and asafoetida. Fill the tomatoes with this mixture. Gently heat the oil in a wok or a large frying pan with a lid. Fry the asafoetida and add the tomatoes and a little water. Give it a quick boil then reduce the heat to the lowest setting. Cover the wok or frying pan and allow the tomatoes to cook until done. When cooked the tomatoes should still be whole. Serve hot with plain rice.

You can also use potatoes, aubergines or okra. Okra will only require a slit. If you use potatoes leave their jackets on and bake them on a greased tray in a moderate oven until done.

Yam Request
Farmaishi Suran
Serves 4–6

When I first tried this it was prepared with fish. I liked the taste very much and I knew I would have to find a substitute for fish. Then I remembered when I was living at home in India my mother used to fry thin slices of yam lightly spiced and as children we often mistook it for fish.

1 bunch coriander leaves, picked and washed
3.75-cm (1½-inch) piece fresh ginger
salt and fresh chillies to taste (I use 4 green chillies)
1 teaspoon cloves
1 teaspoon peppercorns
25g (1 oz) coriander seeds
6 green cardamoms, peeled
350g (12 oz) yam, peeled and thinly sliced
oil for deep-frying
100g (¼ lb) onions, finely sliced
juice of 2 lemons ·
a few saffron strands, dissolved in 2 teaspoons warm milk
a pinch nutmeg
a pinch mace
chopped coriander leaves, to garnish

Grind the coriander leaves, ginger, salt, chillies, cloves, peppercorns, coriander seeds and cardamoms to a fine paste. Marinate yam slices in the paste for 30 minutes. Heat the oil in a deep frying pan or a wok and fry the sliced onions to a golden brown and remove. Remove some of the excess oil and fry the marinated yam slices until evenly brown on all sides. Add the lemon juice and a little water. Cover the wok and allow to simmer gently. When the water has dried and the gravy is of a thick consistency add the fried onions, saffron, nutmeg and mace. Stir well and cook for a further 5 minutes. Serve hot garnished with chopped coriander leaves.

Potato Bake
Dum Aloo
Serves 4

An Indian girlfriend of mine has been living in Switzerland for nearly twenty years and she made this variation of the popular Swiss *rosti*. I normally use chopped green chillies but these are hot and very noticeable with the bland potato. I have therefore suggested you use chilli powder. Try 4 green chillies finely chopped if you have a trained palate for chillies.

3 large potatoes
salt to taste
1 teaspoon chilli powder
a few coriander leaves,
   chopped

pepper to taste
butter for frying

Peel the potatoes and then grate them finely over a bowl of salted cold water. After 20 minutes drain the potatoes well and add salt, chilli powder, coriander leaves and pepper. In a heavy frying pan (I prefer to use a flat-bottomed non-stick wok) dissolve some butter on a low heat and spread the potato mixture to make a thick pancake. Fry until the first side is nice and crisp. Turn over and fry the other side adding more butter if necessary.

Vegetable Cutlets
Sabzi Petis
Serves 4–6 (or more as a snack)

The *Bhori* Muslims always start and end their meals with a sweet dish. After the first sweet dish two or three fried dishes are served before the main course of curry and rice. These kebabs with variations are often prepared as one of the three fried dishes.

400g (14 oz) potatoes	*a handful fresh coriander*
100g (4 oz) French beans	*leaves, chopped*
100g (4 oz) carrots	*juice of 2 lemons*
100g (4 oz) peas	*4 green chillies, finely*
100g (4 oz) cauliflower	*chopped*
1 teaspoon garlic paste (page	*breadcrumbs for coating*
56)	*oil for shallow-frying*
2 teaspoons ginger paste	*lemon wedges*
(page 56)	

Prepare all the vegetables and cut into small pieces. Mix with the garlic and ginger pastes and boil the vegetables in a little water until soft. Drain any excess water. Lightly mash the vegetables then add the coriander leaves, lemon juice and green chillies. Add salt to taste and mix well. Grease your palms and take a little mixture at a time and shape them into thick cutlets. Roll them in breadcrumbs and shallow-fry on a griddle until golden brown on each side. Serve hot with lemon wedges.

Rich Aubergine Curry
Bagara Baingan

Serves 4−6

This is one of the most famous dishes from Deccan. Hot and spicy and extremely delicious, it is often prepared for weddings and festive occasions in large quantities. The cooks sometimes prepare the dish with extra oil several days in advance so that by the day of the feast the spices have matured.

250g (9 oz) small dark purple aubergines

2 tablespoons sesame oil or vegetable oil

½ teaspoon cumin seeds

4 green chillies, slit on one side

2 tablespoons tamarind juice (page 60)

Ingredients to be ground to a fine paste after dry-roasting

½ onion, sliced

¼ small dry coconut or 4 tablespoons browned desiccated coconut

1 teaspoon sesame seeds

1 teaspoon poppy seeds

½ teaspoon coriander seeds

½ teaspoon chilli powder

½ teaspoon salt

a few curry leaves

½ teaspoon ginger paste (page 56)

1 teaspoon garlic paste (page 56)

a handful coriander leaves

1 green chilli

Make two deep cuts in the aubergines leaving the four sections held together only by the stem. Rub a little of the ground paste into each aubergine and keep aside. Heat the oil in a wok or large pan and fry the cumin seeds and green chillies until the cumin seeds are dark in colour. Add the aubergines and quickly fry them for a few minutes. Remove and keep aside. In the same oil add the ground paste and a few drops of water. Cook until the oil separates and the paste becomes aromatic. Return the aubergines to the pan and allow to simmer until nearly done. Add the tamarind juice and stir gently to avoid damaging the aubergines. Continue to simmer until the aubergines are fully done, and the oil shows on the top. Adjust salt if necessary.

Bell Pepper Curry
Mirch ka Salan

Use peppers or large green chillies instead of aubergines. Slit the chillies and remove the seeds. Soak in diluted vinegar and salt for an hour. Cook as above replacing aubergines with peppers or green chillies and omitting the green chilli from the spices.

Bengali Mixed Vegetables 1
Labda
Serves 4−6

One of the two most popular vegetable dishes of Bengal. Blending a range of vegetables and spices the Bengalis obtain an unusual combination of flavours in one dish.

Panch poran is a combination of five (*'panch'*) whole aromatic spices: mustard seeds, cumin seeds, onion seeds, fennel seeds and fenugreek seeds. It is available from Indian grocers.

2 small aubergines
1 ridge gourd, scraped, pith and seeds removed
2 potatoes, washed and quartered
2 carrots
a few cauliflower florets
2 drumsticks, scraped and cut into 5-cm (2-inch) pieces
6−8 whole green beans
2 peppers
a small piece red pumpkin, peeled
1 small sweet potato, peeled
4 tablespoons oil
3 green chillies, slit
3 red chillies, slit
½ teaspoon turmeric powder
½ teaspoon chilli powder
¼ teaspoon coriander powder
¼ teaspoon cumin powder
1 teaspoon panch poran
a pinch sugar
salt to taste

Prepare all the vegetables and cut them into bite-size pieces. Heat the oil in a large pan and fry the green and red chillies for 2 minutes. Reduce the heat and add the remaining spices, sugar and salt. Mix well and add the vegetables. Cover the pan and cook until the vegetables are done and are not separate from one another. If there is excess gravy thicken it with wheatflour or gram flour (*besan* or *channa atta*).

Bengali Mixed Vegetables 2
Shukto
Serves 4–6

Shukto is one of the most popular vegetarian Bengali dishes. Shukto is neither sweet, sour, nor bitter, but all these different tastes merged together.

1 sweet potato, peeled and cubed
2 potatoes, washed and quartered
1 bitter gourd scraped, pith and seeds removed
1 ridge gourd, scraped, pith and seeds removed
100g (4 oz) peas
4 tablespoons oil
¼ teaspoon mustard seeds
2.5-cm (1-inch) piece fresh ginger
½ tablespoon poppy seeds, dry-roasted
½ teaspoon turmeric powder
salt and chilli powder to taste
1½ teaspoons cumin powder
a pinch sugar
2 bay leaves
½ cup milk

Wash and prepare all the vegetables, cutting them into bite-size pieces. Heat the oil in a wok or a large pan and fry each vegetable separately for 5 minutes. Drain and keep aside. Grind the mustard seeds, ginger and poppy seeds. Mix this paste with turmeric powder, salt and chilli powder, cumin powder and sugar. Reheat the oil and on a medium heat fry the spices until the oil separates. Add the vegetables and tuck in the bay leaves. Cover the pan and cook the vegetables until they are soft. Five minutes before cooking time turn off the heat and allow the vegetables to cool slightly. Slowly fold in the milk. Bring back to the boil and serve hot with *luchis* (page 230).

Maharashtran-style Grated Potatoes
Batataya Chi Khis
Serves 4–6

This dish is very delicious when served with any lentil curry. Sweet potatoes can be cooked in the same way. At no stage should any water be added.

3 potatoes
4 tablespoons ghee
1 teaspoon cumin seeds
3 green chillies, finely
  chopped
2 cups peanuts, coarsely
  ground
salt and sugar to taste (if you
  are using salted peanuts be
  careful)

½ cup freshly grated coconut
  or desiccated coconut
a few coriander leaves,
  chopped
juice of 1 lemon

Wash, peel and grate the potato over a bowl of cold salted water. Drain well. In a heavy frying pan or wok heat the ghee and fry the cumin seeds and green chillies. When the seeds turn dark brown add the potato and mix well. When the mixture starts steaming add the ground peanuts, salt and sugar. Mix well. Cover the pan and over a slow heat cook until the potato is done. Garnish with grated coconut and coriander leaves. Sprinkle with lemon juice just before serving.

Nut Cutlets

Serves 4−6 (or more as a snack)

These can be served hot or cold, and are also delicious in baps, like hamburgers. Use either nuts on their own or parboiled vegetables and a few nuts.

15g (½ oz) plain flour
25g (1 oz) butter or
  margarine
150ml (5 fl oz) milk
salt and pepper to taste
a generous pinch powdered
  mace
125g (5 oz) peeled mixed
  nuts

50g (2 oz) onions, finely
  chopped
a handful coriander leaves,
  chopped
1 egg
breadcrumbs for coating
butter or ghee for shallow-
  frying

Make a thick sauce with the flour, butter and milk. Add salt, pepper, and mace. Mix well and keep aside. Coarsely grind the nuts and mix with onions and coriander leaves. Mix the sauce and the nut mixture and adjust seasoning. Allow the mixture to cool. Divide into equal portions and shape on a floured board. Brush with egg and toss in breadcrumbs. Fry quickly in hot butter or ghee. Drain and serve hot.

Cashew Nut Curry
Kaju Ka Salan
Serves 4−6

A light-flavoured dish to include in your menu if you are serving other dishes with a strong flavour.

250g (9 oz) paneer (page
  46)
100g (4 oz) cashew nuts,
  peeled and raw
2 tablespoons oil
2 tablespoons grated coconut,
  or desiccated coconut
2 bay leaves
½ teaspoon sugar

½ teaspoon turmeric powder
1 teaspoon garam masala
salt and chilli powder to taste
100g (4 oz) skinned
  tomatoes, sliced
2 tablespoons natural yogurt
a few coriander leaves,
  chopped, to garnish

Cut the *paneer* into small cubes and fry until they are golden brown on all sides. Drain and keep aside. Wash and soak the cashew nuts in water for 1 hour. Heat 2 tablespoons oil and on a medium heat fry the coconut, bay leaves, sugar, turmeric powder, garam masala, salt and chilli powder. Fry for about 5 minutes then add the tomatoes and yogurt. Drain the cashew nuts and add to the pan. Add a little hot water and cover the pan. Cook until the gravy thickens a little. Add the *paneer* cubes and simmer gently for a further 5 minutes. Garnish with coriander leaves and serve hot.

Rich Vegetable Curry
Sabzi Khorma
Serves 4–6

You will often find *khorma* on the menu in an Indian restaurant which are usually made with meat, poultry and fish. I tried the same recipe with vegetables and it was very delicious.

Vegetables

2 large onions
1½ cups peas
1 small cauliflower, cut into florets
2 small carrots, peeled and diced
2 large potatoes, washed and quartered
2 large unripe tomatoes, quartered
1 small turnip, peeled and cubed
1 teaspoon poppy seeds, dry-roasted
1 teaspoon aniseed, dry-roasted
1 teaspoon sesame seeds, dry-roasted

½ teaspoon turmeric powder
5 green chillies
2.5-cm (1-inch) piece fresh ginger
a generous helping fresh coriander leaves
½ freshly grated coconut or 1 cup desiccated coconut, dry-roasted
2 tablespoons oil
2.5-cm (1-inch) quill cinnamon
2 green cardamoms, bruised, with the peel
4 cloves

Slice one onion and keep aside. Wash and prepare the other vegetables and keep aside. Grind the other onion along with poppy seeds, aniseed, sesame seeds, turmeric powder, chillies, ginger and coriander leaves. Grind the coconut separately. Heat the oil and fry the cinnamon, cardamom and cloves until the cloves swell. Add the sliced onion and sauté until golden brown. Add the ground paste and fry until the oil separates. Add the vegetables and ground coconut and mix well. Add a few drops of water if necessary. Add salt to taste. Cover the pan and cook on a low heat until all the vegetables are done. Serve hot with any bread or rice.

Dry Vegetable Grill
Dum ke Sabzi
Serves 4—6

I enjoy this dish very much particularly during the hot summer months. All the vegetables are crunchy and blend well with the cheese and egg topping.

2 green peppers, cut into bite-size pieces

2 medium-sized ripe tomatoes, quartered

a few French beans, cut into small pieces

2 large potatoes, washed and cubed

2 large carrots, peeled and diced

½ cup shelled peas

salt to taste

½ teaspoon chilli powder

pepper to taste

1 tablespoon grated cheese

4 eggs

Blanch the prepared vegetables in boiling salted water for 2 minutes. Drain well and arrange them in a greased pie dish. Sprinkle salt, chilli powder and pepper to taste. Sprinkle the grated cheese over evenly (add more if you wish). Carefully break the eggs on top. Sprinkle some more salt and pepper. Bake in a moderately hot oven until the eggs have set. Serve hot.

Dry Mixed Vegetable
Sabzi Jal Frazi
Serves 4–6

In my home in India we always have a vegetable dish with chappatis as the first course and then move on to other curries and rice. The following recipe is how my mother prepared this dish.

oil for deep-frying
6 small potatoes, washed and
   halved
2 onions, sliced
2 carrots, peeled and diced
1 cup peas
1 small turnip, peeled and
   cubed
1 tomato, quartered
a few French beans, cut in
   2.5-cm (1-inch) pieces
1 clove garlic, crushed

2.5-cm (1-inch) piece fresh
   ginger, crushed
6 red chillies, seeded and
   finely chopped
1 teaspoon black pepper
1 teaspoon garam masala
½ teaspoon turmeric powder
salt to taste
cucumber slices, mint leaves
   and lemon wedges, to
   garnish

Heat the oil in a wok or deep frying pan and fry the potatoes till well browned. Drain and keep aside. Remove excess oil leaving about 3 tablespoons in the wok or pan. Heat the oil and fry the onions until golden brown. Add the remaining vegetables and fry for 5 minutes stirring constantly. Add the remaining ingredients, potatoes and salt to taste. Add a little hot water if necessary. (I like to add the least amount of water as possible. To avoid the vegetables burning cover your pan with a pyrex plate and put some cold water in it. If you are using a wok put some water in the hollow where the knob is.) Mix well. Cover the pan and allow the vegetables to cook until done and the gravy is almost dry. Garnish and serve hot with chappatis and freshly made natural yogurt.

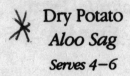

Dry Potato
Aloo Sag
Serves 4−6

I learnt this from my maid who is an Andhra Pradesh Hindu. It is served with *dosai* (page 68) but also makes a delicious sandwich filling.

4 large potatoes
salt
4 tablespoons oil
2 large onions, chopped
2 green chillies, finely chopped
a handful coriander leaves, finely chopped
½ teaspoon turmeric powder

½ teaspoon mustard seeds
2 dried red chillies, seeded and coarsely crushed
a few curry leaves, coarsely chopped
juice of 2 lemons
finely chopped spring onions, to garnish

Wash and peel the potatoes and cut them in small pieces. Boil them in salted water until cooked. Drain well and coarsely mash them. Keep aside. In a wok or a large frying pan heat the oil and fry the onions until they are soft. Add the green chillies, coriander leaves, turmeric powder, mustard seeds, curry leaves and salt to taste. Mix well and keep frying on a low heat for about 5 minutes. Add a few drops of water and fold in the potato mixing well to ensure the even distribution of the spices. Just before serving mix in the lemon juice. I like to garnish this dish with finely chopped spring onions.

White Vegetable Curry
Hussainy Sabzi
Serves 4–6

This is yet another meat curry popular in Hyderabad. I have omitted the meat and substituted *paneer* in its place. You can cook it on top of the stove or as a casserole in the oven and serve with plain bread or seasoned mashed potatoes.

250g (9 oz) paneer (page 46)
oil for shallow-frying
2 large potatoes, washed and cubed
6 shallots, peeled and trimmed
1 carrot, peeled and diced
4 small courgettes, diced
1 cup peas
salt
a few beans of any kind
1 large onion, finely chopped
½ teaspoon turmeric powder
1 teaspoon chilli powder (or to taste)

½ teaspoon cumin powder
6 cloves garlic, finely crushed or 1 heaped teaspoon garlic paste (page 56)
5-cm (2-inch) piece fresh ginger, finely crushed, or ½ teaspoon ginger paste (page 56)
6 green chillies, finely chopped
3 large tomatoes, quartered
75ml (3 fl oz) natural yogurt, beaten
juice of 1 lemon
a few mint leaves, to garnish

Cut the *paneer* into cubes and fry in oil in a non-stick frying pan or a wok until well browned. Remove and keep aside. Parboil the potatoes, shallots, carrot, courgettes, peas and beans in salted water. Drain and keep aside. Heat 4 tablespoons oil in the wok and fry the onions till golden brown. While the onions are frying mix the turmeric powder, chilli powder, cumin powder, garlic, ginger, chillies and salt with a little water. When the onions are brown add the mixed spice paste and fry on a low heat until the oil separates. Return the vegetables to the wok along with the tomatoes and gradually add the yogurt, stirring continuously. Cook until the vegetables are done and there is a thick gravy. Just before serving add the lemon juice and garnish with the fried *paneer* and mint leaves.

Potatoes and Peas in Yogurt
Dahi Aloo Mattar

Serves 4—6 (or more as a starter)

Vegetables in yogurt are always my favourite. Serve this dish as part of a main meal or as a starter. If you are serving it as a starter it can be served either hot or cold.

*450g (1 lb) small new
  potatoes
1 tablespoon ghee or oil
1½ teaspoons cumin seeds,
  dry-roasted
½ teaspoon turmeric powder
1 teaspoon coriander powder
a pinch asafoetida*

*1 cup peas
¾ pint (450ml) thick natural
  yogurt, beaten
salt to taste
1 teaspoon garam masala
a handful coriander leaves,
  chopped*

Wash the potatoes well and boil them in salted water until done. (I leave the jackets on but if you wish you can cool the potatoes a little and then peel them.) Heat the ghee in a wok or a large frying pan and fry the cumin seeds. When they crackle add the turmeric powder, coriander powder and asafoetida. Reduce the heat and add the potatoes and peas. Gradually add the yogurt and salt to taste. Cook on a very slow heat for about 10 minutes. When the gravy thickens remove from the heat and serve garnished with garam masala and coriander leaves.

Pumpkin with Creamed Yogurt
Lal Kaddu Chakka
Serves 4–6

Pumpkin as a vegetable has never had the same recognition as other seasonals like cauliflower, cabbage, peas, for example.

FOR CHAKKA

1 teaspoon powdered
  cardamom

6 cups thick natural yogurt
salt

FOR PUMPKIN

450g (1 lb) pumpkin, peeled,
  seeded and cut into thin
  slices or grated
4 tablespoons oil
2 large onions, finely sliced
2 teaspoons chilli powder, or
  to taste

1 teaspoon coriander powder
2 tablespoons pomegranate
  seeds, powdered, or juice of
  1 lemon
¼ teaspoon turmeric powder
salt to taste

To garnish
grated coconut
fresh coriander leaves,
  chopped

tomatoes, chopped

Mix the cardamom powder with the yogurt and tie in a muslin cloth. Hang it over a bowl to collect the whey for 4–5 hours or until only the cream is left behind. Knead well and add salt to taste. Lightly crumble the cream of the yogurt and place it in a serving dish. Smear the pumpkin with some salt and keep aside. Heat the oil in a wok or frying pan and fry the onions until golden brown. Add the remaining spices and salt to taste. Drain the pumpkin well, add to the spices and mix well. Cover the wok and allow the pumpkin to cook until fully done. Place the pumpkin on the *chakka*, garnish and serve.

Gypsy or Cluster Bean Curry
Guvar Ki Phalli
Serves 4—6

When I was working for Air-India five of us girls ate together at lunch time. We began by buying sandwiches but soon got fed up. One of the girls then took on the responsibility of providing us with lunch everyday. Her mother prepared this dish as a dry curry and used it as a sandwich filling. Lunches were never boring again as each day she sent us something different. Most of the recipes in this book which are dry-based make excellent sandwich fillings.

4 tablespoons oil
1 large onion, finely chopped
2.5-cm (1-inch) piece fresh ginger, crushed
4 cloves garlic, crushed
1 teaspon cumin powder
2 teaspoons coriander powder
½ teaspoon turmeric powder
2 teaspoons chilli powder, or to taste .

salt to taste
225g (8 oz) gypsy or cluster beans (guvar), stringed and cut into 2.5-cm (1-inch) pieces
100g (4 oz) chunky soya meat
2 tablespoons tomato purée
coriander leaves

Heat the oil in a heavy pan and fry the onion until golden brown in colour. Add the ginger and garlic and continue frying until the raw smell disappears. Add the powdered spices and salt and fry until the oil separates. Add the beans and soya with a little hot water. Mix well. Cover the pan and allow to simmer until the beans are done and the soya meat has absorbed the water and become soft. Add the tomato purée and coriander leaves. Simmer for 2—3 minutes more. Serve cold as a sandwich filling or hot with *kitchdi* (page 99) and a yogurt *raitha* (pages 208–11).

Aubergine and Red Gram Curry
Vaingya Ambot
Serves 4–6

The following two recipes come from a very good Goanese friend of mine who lives in Bombay. Goa, now known as Panjim, has been restored to India by the Portuguese but their influence on the food will remain for a long time. Their food is hot so adjust the chillies accordingly.

2 large, dark purple aubergines

1 cup red gram (tuvar *or* arhar dhal*)*

1 large onion, sliced

4 tablespoons tamarind juice (page 60)

Ingredients to be dry roasted and ground

¼ coconut, grated, or ¼ cup desiccated coconut

10 dried red chillies, or to taste

½ teaspoon turmeric powder

1 tablespoon coriander seeds

Ingredients for final fry (*tarka*) (page 49)

2 tablespoons oil

1 onion, finely sliced

a generous pinch asafoetida

1 teaspoon mustard seeds

Cut the aubergines into bite-size pieces and place them in cold salted water. Wash the gram and place in a large heavy pan with 1 cup water. Bring to the boil and then simmer until the gram is half cooked. Add the aubergines and sliced onion together with the ground masala. Cook until both the gram and the vegetable are cooked. Add the tamarind juice and boil for 5 minutes. In a small frying pan heat the oil and fry the mustard seeds and asafoetida until the mustard seeds crackle. Add the sliced onion and fry until they are golden brown. Immediately add to the main pan and cover it immediately. Serve hot with a rice dish.

Goanese Potato
Batata Bhaji
Serves 4−6

A very tangy dish. I tasted it when we were invited to go on a picnic with my Goanese friend. Sitting in the beautiful Hanging Gardens in Bombay her maid served each person with some of this potato dish, crusty bread and a crisp salad.

450g (1 lb) small, round new potatoes, washed and left whole
salt

4 tablespoons oil
1 cup peas
2 tablespoons tomato purée
a handful coriander leaves

Ingredients to be ground together
6 tablespoons desiccated coconut, dry-roasted
6 dried red chillies, dry-roasted
2 teaspoons coriander powder
2 medium-sized onions, dry-roasted

2 teaspoons poppy seeds, dry-roasted
1 teaspoon five-spice powder
5 cloves garlic, dry-roasted

Boil the potatoes in salted water until they are nearly done. Drain the water leaving the potatoes in the same pan. Return the pan to the heat and quickly dry the potatoes in the pan without breaking them. Leave aside. Heat the oil in a large pan and fry the ground paste until the raw smell disappears and the oil separates. Add the peas, tomato purée, salt and coriander leaves and mix well. Add a few drops of water if necessary and simmer until the peas are cooked. Add the potatoes and mix well to coat them evenly. Cook until they are fully done. Serve hot with rice and a lentil curry or cool and serve as above.

Creamed Vegetables
Sabzi Makhanwalla
Serves 4–6 (or more as a starter)

Until I was twelve years old I was allowed to go swimming in a mixed crowd. Among them was an Iranian friend who now owns a restaurant and this dish was on his menu. I must admit he was stout and each time he was about to enter the pool we teased him by saying that the pool would become empty of water but filled with him. This dish is high in calories but is so delicious that perhaps you can indulge in it occasionally.

4 tablespoons oil	*1 large onion, chopped*
3 potatoes, washed, peeled and quartered	*1 cup single cream*
	2 tablespoons plain flour
100g (4 oz) each: beans, cauliflower, carrots and peas	*1 cup milk*
	4 tablespoons tomato ketchup
	½ teaspoon chilli powder
salt	*pepper to taste*
2 tablespoons butter	*mint leaves to garnish*

Heat the oil in a frying pan and sauté the potatoes until evenly browned. Drain and keep aside. Prepare the beans, cauliflower, carrots and peas and boil them in salted water until they are half done. Drain and keep aside. Heat the butter in a wok or large pan and fry the onion until golden brown. Mix the cream, flour, milk, ketchup, chilli powder, salt and pepper to a smooth consistency. Reduce the heat and add the cream mixture gradually, stirring continuously. Add all the vegetables and cook gently until they are done. Garnish with mint leaves and serve hot.

Pulses

Dhal is whole gram split into halves with the husk removed. In various forms it is one of the most important and popular of Indian foods, especially for the vegetarian since it is high in protein. Protein-filled pulses are an essential part of everyday meals and inexpensive too. Split peas, gram, dry beans, *masoor, arhar, moong* and other *dhals* can be turned into a variety of different dishes. Sprouted pulses supply invaluable vitamin B and E and also a fair amount of vitamin A and C. In the south of India, the very act of serving *dhal* is considered auspicious and no wedding, ancestral anniversary, feast or festival will be without *arhar* or *tuwar dhal* (red gram) and *moong dhal* (green gram). *Dhals* are made into sumptuous dishes including savouries, snacks and sweetmeats.

Green Gram Balls
Moong Koftas
Serves 4—6

My favourite Choti Khala ('small aunt') is a Theosophist and therefore a pure vegetarian. She has great faith in all the pulses and this is her recipe for a healthy and a substantial dish.

1 cup whole green gram
(moong)
oil for deep-frying
4 tablespoons ghee or oil
1 small onion, finely chopped
a pinch asafoetida
1 teaspoon cumin seeds
2 ripe tomatoes, chopped
a small bunch coriander
leaves, finely chopped (keep
a few aside for garnish)

2 green chillies, chopped
½ teaspoon turmeric powder
2 teaspoons coriander
powder
½ teaspoon chilli powder
(optional)
1 teaspoon garam masala
(pages 54–6)
salt to taste

Pick and wash the *moong*. Cover with water and allow to soak overnight. Next day wash them in fresh water and remove any loosened husk. Drain well and grind to a fine paste in an electric blender. Heat enough oil for deep-frying in a *karai* or wok and drop in spoonfuls of the *moong* paste to form small balls. Fry them to a golden colour. Drain well and keep aside.

Heat the ghee or oil in a large pan and fry the chopped onions until they are golden brown in colour. Add the asafoetida and cumin seeds along with the tomatoes and the coriander leaves. Mix the remaining ingredients except the *moong koftas* in a little water and add to the pan. Mix well and on a reduced heat fry until the oil separates. Add 1 cup water and bring to the boil. Reduce the heat and simmer for 5 minutes. Add the *moong koftas* and simmer for a further 5 minutes. Garnish with coriander leaves and serve hot with chappatis or plain boiled rice.

Green Gram Soup
Moong Dhal Sherwa
Serves 4–6

This is a very nutritious soup and ideal for someone who has lost their appetite.

½ cup green gram (moong dhal)
4 cups water
½ teaspoon turmeric powder

salt to taste
1 tablespoon ghee or oil
½ teaspoon cumin seeds

Pick and wash the *dhal* and place it in a heavy pan. Add the water, turmeric powder and salt. Bring to the boil, then reduce the heat and simmer until the *dhal* is absolutely tender and the water has reduced by half. Mix well and allow the *dhal* to settle at the bottom of the pan. Remove from the heat and gently pour off the *dhal* liquid. Heat the ghee or oil in a small frying pan and fry the cumin seeds. When the seeds are aromatic pour the oil and seeds over the *dhal* water. Reheat the soup and serve hot with some drops of lemon juice if you wish.

The strained *dhal* is delicious when eaten with a little chopped onion, coriander leaves and lemon juice. Alternatively, do not strain and serve with a little boiled rice cooked to a mushy consistency.

☀ Lentil Soup
Masoor Sherwa
Serves 4–6

Another delicious way of serving lentils. It is particularly nice on a cold winter's evening.

1 tablespoon ghee
3 small onions, sliced
4 cloves garlic
½ teaspoon chilli powder
3 level teaspoons curry powder (page 52)
1 cup red lentils (masoor dhal), *picked, washed and drained*

½ cup cooked rice
3 tomatoes
salt to taste
6 cups water
juice of 1 lemon
coriander leaves for garnish

Heat the ghee in a large pan and fry the onions until soft. Add the garlic, chilli powder and curry powder and fry on a lower heat. Add the remaining ingredients except the lemon juice and coriander leaves. Bring to the boil, then reduce the heat and cook until the *dhal* is soft and mushy. Pass the soup through a sieve using a wooden spoon to help mash the *dhal* and rice. Reheat the *dhal*, add the lemon juice and garnish with the coriander leaves.

If you keep the rice separate and add it to the soup after it has been passed through the sieve and reheated, this adds body to the dish.

Savoury Chickpeas
Kabuli Channa
Serves 4−6

A lovely dish when served with hot pitta bread. As an accompaniment to this you can boil and mash potatoes, mix in chopped green chillies and chopped coriander leaves and salt to taste. Make them in thick patties and dip them in beaten eggs and shallow-fry until they are golden brown and crisp on both sides.

225g (8 oz) chickpeas (kabuli channa)
salt to taste
8−10 large dried red chillies (reduce or seed to suit your taste)
2.5-cm (1-inch) piece dry mango (amchur)
2 teaspoons coriander powder

1 teaspoon cumin powder
1 onion, finely chopped
½ white radish (mooli), *grated*
4 green chillies, seeded and chopped
coriander leaves for garnish

Pick and wash the *channa* and soak them overnight. Change the water and cover them with fresh water. Bring to the boil, then reduce the heat and allow the *channa* to simmer until soft. Add salt to taste. By the time the *channa* has softened all the water should be absorbed. Dry-roast the red chillies and dry mango and grind them to a fine powder. Add to the *channa* with the remaining ingredients except the coriander leaves. Serve hot or cold.

You can cook the *channa* in a pressure cooker (using less water) and this will reduce the cooking time considerably. Boiled *kabuli channa* is available in tins and can be found at all Indian grocers and some supermarkets. If you use this no soaking or boiling is necessary.

Red Gram Curry
Maharashtran Amti
Serves 4—6

Maharashtrans from the hilly regions are pure vegetarians. Their food is light and not too highly spiced. A typical meal consists of rice, *amti, koshumbri* (page 253), chappatis, yogurt or buttermilk and perhaps a sweet. The meal is served on a *thali* — a large round plate with several *katories* — tiny bowls. The *thali* is placed on the floor and the person sits opposite it on a *paat* — a wooden plank.

1 cup red gram (tuvar *or*
  arhar dhal*)*
2 cups water
4 tablespoons oil
1 teaspoon cumin seeds
a pinch asafoetida
1 teaspoon mustard seeds
½ teaspoon turmeric powder

½ teaspoon chilli powder
1 teaspoon goda masala
  (page 53)
a few curry leaves
tamarind, the size of a lime
2 teaspoons light brown
  sugar
salt to taste

In a large pan cook the *dhal* in water until soft and mushy. Using a potato masher or a wooden spoon mash the *dhal* to a smooth consistency. In a frying pan heat the oil and fry the cumin seeds, asafoetida, mustard seeds, turmeric powder, chilli powder and goda masala. When the mustard seeds start to crackle add the curry leaves and fry till they are slightly burnt. Add the oil and the spices to the *dhal* and cover the pan immediately. Soak the tamarind in 1 cup hot water and when soft strain out the juice through a fine sieve. Add the tamarind juice, sugar and salt to the *dhal* and mix well. Reheat the *dhal* and serve hot. If it is too thick add a little more water before reheating.

Black-eyed Beans with Potato
Lobia Alu
Serves 4—6

Lobia beans are beige and kidney-shaped with a distinctive dark dot. My Achi Khala ('good aunt') makes this dish with such perfection that I feel no one else makes *channa alu* like her. I have used *lobia* but you can also use *chole* or chickpeas. Chickpeas are heart-shaped and have a dark brown skin. Both these are readily available at supermarkets and health-food shops.

225g (8 oz) lobia *or* chole
50g (2 oz) *bengal gram* (channa dhal)
1 pint (600ml) water
1 teaspoon salt
¼ teaspoon bicarbonate of soda
1 teaspoon five-spice powder
a pinch asafoetida
1 onion, chopped
2.5-cm (1-inch) piece fresh ginger, crushed
10 mint leaves
4 tablespoons oil
½ teaspoon turmeric powder

½ teaspoon coriander powder
½ teaspoon cumin powder
½ teaspoon chilli powder (or to taste)
75ml (3 fl oz) tamarind juice (page 60)
2 potatoes, boiled, peeled and cubed
½ bunch coriander leaves, coarsely chopped
2 medium-sized firm tomatoes, chopped
lemon wedges

Pick and wash the *dhals* and soak them overnight. Drain them and place them in a heavy pan or a pressure cooker. Add the water, salt, bicarbonate, five-spice powder, asafoetida, onion, ginger and mint leaves. Cook until the *dhals* are soft. Keep aside. Heat the oil in a large frying pan and on a medium heat fry the turmeric, coriander, cumin and chilli powder. Add the tamarind juice and continue frying until the raw tamarind smell disappears. Add the potatoes and drained *dhals* and mix well. Simmer until a thick gravy forms. Adjust seasoning. Serve hot, garnished with coriander leaves, tomato and lemon wedges. This dish should have a distinctive, sour taste, and *bhatura* (page 237) makes a nice accompaniment.

Simple Lentil Curry
Masoor Dhal
Serves 4–6

My mother's version of a simple lentil curry, and she would often cook sweet saffron rice to serve with it. Yes, a strange savoury and sweet combination, but be brave and try it as it is truly unusual and yet delicious.

1 cup lentils (masoor dhal)	*a few coriander leaves*
½ teaspoon turmeric powder	*2 tablespoons ghee or oil*
2 green chillies, left whole	*½ onion, finely sliced*
3 cloves garlic, finely chopped	*salt to taste*

Pick and wash the *dhal*. In a heavy pan cook with 2 cups water, turmeric powder, green chillies, garlic and coriander leaves. When most of the water has evaporated mash the *dhal* and add more water if necessary to give it the consistency of a thick pea soup. Fry the onion in the oil until crisp and brown and immediately add to the *dhal*. Serve hot with chappatis or plain rice.

If you prepare this a while before you are serving check the consistency as all pulses absorb water. Add some more water if necessary, reboil and serve. You can also serve this as a soup but make the consistency slightly thinner and add lemon juice and a pinch of sugar.

Spiced Lentil Curry
Masala Dhal
Serves 4–6

If you have tried the previous recipe and enjoyed it try this one
which has a few more spices added to make it even tastier.

1 cup red gram (arhar or
tuvar dhal)
10 green chillies, seeded or
reduced to suit your taste
½ teaspoon turmeric powder
salt to taste
3 large tomatoes, quartered

½ cup grated coconut or
desiccated coconut
2 tablespoons ghee or oil
¼ teaspoon mustard seeds
½ teaspoon cumin seeds
a handful coriander leaves,
chopped

Pick and wash the *dhal*. Place in a large heavy pan with 2 cups
water, turmeric powder and green chillies. Bring to the boil
and then reduce the heat and allow to simmer until the *dhal* is
soft and mushy. Keep a careful watch as lentils tend to boil
over. When the *dhal* is soft and mushy most of the water
should have evaporated. Using a wooden spoon mix it into a
smooth consistency. Add salt to taste, tomatoes and coconut.
Heat the ghee in a small frying pan and fry the mustard and
cumin seeds. When the mustard seeds begin to crackle,
immediately pour the oil and spices over the *dhal* and cover
the pan to retain the aroma. Garnish with coriander leaves and
serve hot with rice or chappatis.

Sprouted Green Gram
Phule Moong
Serves 4–6

Sprouted pulses are easier to digest because the germination process converts the starch to dextrose and maltose. This makes them suitable for anyone with digestive problems.

*225g (8 oz) whole green
  gram* (moong)
2 tablespoons ghee or oil
2 cloves
a pinch asafoetida
½ teaspoon turmeric powder

1 teaspoon coriander powder
chilli powder to taste
salt to taste
1 teaspoon amchur *(dry
  mango powder)*
lemon juice

Pick and wash the *moong* and cover them with water. Leave them to soak for a few hours. Drain well and wrap them in a wet cloth. Leave covered overnight if the weather is cold or remove as soon as the *dhal* starts to sprout. Wash the sprouted *dhal* in cold water and drain well. Heat the oil in a heavy pan. Reduce the heat and fry the cloves and asafoetida. When the cloves swell and rise, add the sprouted *moong* and stir-fry for a few minutes. Add the turmeric, coriander and chilli powders and salt to taste. Mix well. Add a little water, cover the pan and allow the *moong* to cook until tender but not mushy. When all the water is absorbed and the *moong* tender sprinkle *amchur* powder and lemon juice to taste and mix well.

If you are unable to find *amchur* then increase the lemon juice to suit your taste. Serve hot with pitta bread.

Moghul Dhal
Shahjahani Dhal
Serves 4—6

Moghlai cookery conjures up visions of sumptuous banquets against a luxurious backdrop. The richness of the food may be hard on the budget, so this recipe would come in the category to be filed away for special occasions.

Khova can be purchased from Indian sweet shops or made at home. It does require a lot of time and patience but the effort will be worth it. To make 125g (4 oz) *khova* you will need 1.2 litres (2 pints) of rich creamy milk. Bring the milk to the boil and then reduce the heat and simmer until the milk is thick. When the milk begins to reach a doughy consistency sprinkle in a few drops of lemon juice. This will give the *khova* a flaky texture. It has to be stirred constantly to prevent it from boiling over or sticking to the bottom of the pan. This can take anything between 2—4 hours.

225g (8 oz) bengal gram
 (channa dhal)
3 tablespoons ghee
4 cloves
1 quill cinnamon
2 cardamoms
1 onion, finely sliced

½ cup thick coconut milk
 (pages 58–60)
100g (4 oz) khova
salt to taste
2 green chillies, sliced
flesh from ¼ fresh coconut,
 cut into small cubes

Place the *dhal* in a large heavy pan and cover with water. Bring to the boil and then reduce the heat and allow to simmer until the *dhal* is parboiled. Remove from the heat. In another saucepan heat the ghee and when it begins to smoke put in the whole spices and fry for 30 seconds. Add the sliced onions and fry them until golden brown. Add the *dhal* with the water and continue to simmer for about 10 minutes. Add the coconut milk and mix well. Leave the pan uncovered and simmer until most of the liquid in the pan has evaporated. Add the *khova*, salt and coconut cubes and stir well. Cook until there is a thick gravy. Serve hot with *puris*.

Red Gram Curry
Tuvar Dhal

Serves 4–6

2 cups red gram (arhar or
  tuvar dhal), *picked and
  washed*
4 tablespoons ghee or oil
4 green chillies, slit
a few curry leaves
1 tablespoon cumin seeds
1 tablespoon fenugreek seeds
1 teaspoon turmeric powder
salt to taste
1 teaspoon chilli powder (or
  to taste)

4 drumsticks (moringa),
  peeled and cut into 5-cm
  (2-inch) pieces
100g (4 oz) whole green
  beans, cut into 5-cm (2-
  inch) pieces
a handful fresh coriander
  leaves, chopped
1 tablespoon sugar
100g (4 oz) okra, left whole
juice of 1 lemon

Place the *dhal* in a large heavy pan and add 4 cups water. Bring to the boil and then reduce the heat and cook the *dhal* until it is soft and mushy. When all the water has been absorbed mash the *dhal* with a wooden spoon or a potato masher until you have a smooth, thick-soup-like consistency. In a separate large pan heat the ghee or oil and fry the green chillies, curry leaves, cumin seeds, fenugreek seeds and stir until the chillies whiten. Add the turmeric powder, salt, chilli powder, coriander powder and the vegetables and stir-fry for about 5 minutes. Add the mashed *dhal* and mix well. If the gravy is too thick add a little warm water and simmer until the vegetables are cooked. Just before serving add the lemon juice and the coriander leaves. Serve hot with plain boiled rice or *bagare chawal* (page 000).

Bengal Gram Salad
Channa Dhal Salad

Serves 4—6

My family always enjoys salads and this one makes a welcome change from the usual tossed salads. Serve as an accompaniment to the main meal or as an individual starter.

1 cup bengal gram (channa
 dhal), *picked, washed and
 soaked overnight*
1 cucumber
salt to taste
4 green chillies (or to taste)
½ bunch coriander leaves
*4 tablespoons desiccated
 coconut*

juice of ½ lemon
1 tablespoon oil
½ teaspoon mustard seeds
a pinch asafoetida
¼ teaspoon turmeric powder
a few lettuce leaves
2 firm tomatoes
lemon wedges

Cook the *dhal* in a little water until tender but not mushy. Drain and keep aside. Cut the cucumber into 5-cm (2-inch) pieces and then cut each piece in half lengthways. Scoop out the pulp and keep aside. Sprinkle the cucumber pieces with some salt and keep aside. Grind the chillies, coriander leaves and coconut using the lemon juice to facilitate the grinding. Heat the oil in a frying pan and on a medium heat fry the mustard seeds, asafoetida and turmeric powder until the mustard seeds start to crackle. Lower the heat and add the ground chilli mixture and fry for 1 minute. Add the oil and spices to the *dhal* and mix well. (If you wish you can fold the cucumber pulp into the *dhal*.) Add salt if necessary. Cover a serving platter with lettuce leaves. Pile the *dhal* mixture into the cucumber scoops and place them on the lettuce leaves. Garnish with tomato slices and lemon wedges, chill and serve.

Vegetables and Pulses (Parsi Style)
Sabzi Dhansak
Serves 4–6

Traditional Parsis would curl up at the thought of preparing this dish without some sort of meat. But I was once asked to produce vegetarian *dhansak* for a sports club occasion and, although I was too embarrassed to let it be known that I was responsible for the dish, it was really quite delicious and it proved that meat is not an essential ingredient. This is a festive dish among the Parsis in India and is served with seasoned rice, *bund gobhi* kebabs (page 130) and a salad made from chopped onions, tomatoes, coriander leaves and green peppers. When pumpkins are out of season, use carrots.

175g (6 oz) red gram (arhar or tuvar dhal)
50g (2 oz) bengal gram (channa)
50g (2 oz) green gram (moong dhal)
50g (2 oz) red lentils (masoor dhal)
4 mint leaves
1 pint (600ml) water
1 aubergine, cut into pieces and soaked in cold water
2 potatoes, peeled, cut into large pieces and soaked in cold water
4 onions, finely sliced
100g (4 oz) spinach or fenugreek (methi bhaji)
100g (4 oz) pumpkin, peeled and cut into large pieces
½ bunch coriander leaves
5 green chillies, chopped and seeded for a milder flavour
2.5-cm (1-inch) piece fresh ginger, crushed
3 cloves garlic, crushed
oil for frying
1 teaspoon cumin powder
2 teaspoons coriander powder
½ teaspoon clove powder
½ teaspoon cinnamon powder
1 teaspoon turmeric powder
1 teaspoon chilli powder (optional)
2 bay leaves
salt to taste
a pinch sugar

185

Pick and wash all the *dhals* and allow them to soak for about 30 minutes. Place in a heavy pan with the mint leaves and water. Add the aubergine, potato, spinach and pumpkin. Bring to the boil and then simmer until all the *dhals* are soft and mushy. Mash with a potato masher. Add a little hot water if the consistency is too thick. In a frying pan heat the oil and fry the onion until golden brown. Keep aside some onion slices for garnishing. Add half the coriander leaves, green chillies, ginger and garlic. Fry for 2–3 minutes on a lower heat. Add the powdered spices, bay leaves, salt and sugar. Add all the fried ingredients with the oil to the *dhal* and return the *dhal* pan to the heat. Simmer for a further 10 minutes. Garnish with the reserved onion and coriander leaves.

South Indian Lentil Curry

Sambhar

Serves 4–6

A favourite south Indian dish, mainly eaten as a second course. It is prepared daily and there are many variations. *Sambhar* is a thick sauce which is either plain or made with vegetables and it is eaten with plain boiled rice, *idlis* (page 69) and *dosai* (page 68). Red gram *(arhar* or *tuvar dhal)* and tamarind are essential ingredients.

½ cup red gram (arhar or tuvar dhal) *picked and washed*
2 cups water
½ teaspoon turmeric powder
1 teaspoon oil
4 tablespoons tamarind juice (page 60)

salt to taste
1 tablespoon coriander powder
2 dried red chillies
¼ cup desiccated coconut

Ingredients for final fry (*tarka*) (page 49)

2 tablespoons oil	*1 dried red chilli*
½ teaspoon mustard seeds	*a pinch asafoetida*
¼ teaspoon fenugreek seeds	*a few curry leaves*

In a large heavy pan place the *dhal*, water, turmeric powder and oil. Bring to the boil and then simmer till the *dhal* is soft and mushy. Mash with a wooden spoon or potato masher. Add the tamarind juice and salt to taste. If the curry is too thick add a little warm water to obtain the consistency of a pea soup. Dry-roast the coriander seeds, chillies and coconut until the coconut is golden brown in colour. Grind in a blender or in a pestle and mortar. Add the ground mixture to the *dhal* and mix well. Heat the remaining oil in a frying pan and when nearly smoking add the *tarka* ingredients and fry until the mustard seeds begin to crackle. Pour the oil and spices over the *dhal* and cover the pan immediately to retain the aroma. Serve hot.

You can also add vegetables of your choice. Add 225g (8 oz) mixed vegetables when you have mashed the *dhal*. Cook until the vegetables are done. Then add the tamarind juice and salt and do the final fry. Commonly used vegetables in India are gourds, aubergine, okra, potato, sweet potato, shallots, kholrabi, peppers and *mooli* (white radish).

Lentil with Spinach Curry
Hara Sambhar

Serves 4–6

1 cup red gram (arhar or
  tuvar dhal)*, picked and
  washed*
*225g (8 oz) frozen chopped
  spinach, thawed*
*4 tablespoons tamarind juice
  (page 60)*

*2 green chillies (seeded for a
  milder flavour)*
salt to taste
*a handful fresh coriander
  leaves, coarsely chopped*

Ingredients for final fry *(tarka)* (page 49)
2 tablespoons oil
a pinch asafoetida
½ teaspoon mustard seeds
½ teaspoon cumin seeds

2 dried red chillies
½ teaspoon turmeric powder
2 cloves garlic, sliced
a few curry leaves

In a heavy pan cook the *dhal* with 3 cups water until soft and
mushy. Mash with a wooden spoon or potato masher until you
have a smooth consistency. Add the spinach, tamarind juice,
green chillies and salt to taste and mix well. Heat the oil in a
frying pan and fry the *tarka* ingredients until the mustard
seeds begin to crackle and the garlic is golden brown.
Immediately pour the oil and the spices over the *dhal* and
cover the pan. Simmer the *dhal* for 5−8 minutes to cook the
spinach. Serve hot, garnishing with coriander leaves.

Lentil and Onion Curry
Piyaz Sambhar
Serves 4–6

200g (7 oz) red gram (arhar or tuvar dhal), *picked and washed*

225g (8 oz) shallots, peeled and left whole

4 drumsticks (moringa), scraped and cut into 5-cm (2-inch) pieces

4 tablespoons tamarind juice (page 60)

3 green chillies

a pinch sugar

salt to taste

a handful coriander leaves

Ingredients to be roasted in a few drops of oil and ground

1 tablespoon desiccated coconut

1 teaspoon bengal gram (channa dhal)

1 teaspoon black gram (urad dhal)

4 dried red chillies (seeded for a milder flavour)

Ingredients for final fry (*tarka*) (page 49)

4 tablespoons oil

1 teaspoon mustard seeds

a few curry leaves

In a heavy pan cook the *dhal* with 3 cups of water until soft and mushy. Mash with a wooden spoon or potato masher until you have a smooth consistency. Add the shallots, drumsticks, tamarind juice, chillies, sugar, salt and ground ingredients. Mix well. If too thick add a little warm water. Simmer the *dhal* until the onions and drumsticks are cooked. Heat the oil in a frying pan and fry the *tarka* ingredients until the mustard seeds begin to crackle. Immediately pour the oil and spices over the *dhal* and cover the pan. Serve hot, garnishing with coriander leaves.

If you have difficulty in obtaining drumsticks use okra, aubergine, marrow or pumpkin.

Lentil Water Curry with Bottle Gourd
Palida
Serves 4–6

Dhal chawal (page 105) should always be served with *palida*. If you have difficulty in obtaining bottle gourd use marrow or courgettes. In India we use *kokum* (dry basil flowers) to make this dish sour, but lemon juice has the same effect.

4 tablespoons oil
¼ teaspoon fenugreek seeds
2 cloves garlic, crushed
1 teaspoon coriander powder
1 teaspoon cumin powder
1 teaspoon chilli powder (or to taste)
4 tablespoons bengal gram flour (channa atta *or* besan)

dhal *water (reserved from* dhal chawal *recipe)*
450g (1 lb) bottle gourd (kaddu), *peeled, pith and seeds removed, and cut into bite-size pieces*
½ cup tomato juice
lemon juice to taste
salt to taste
a handful coriander leaves

Heat the oil in a large pan and fry the fenugreek seeds until aromatic. Reduce heat and add garlic, coriander, cumin and chilli powder and fry for 2 minutes. Add the gram flour and fry again for 2 minutes. Add the *dhal* water and mix well until there are no lumps. Add the bottle gourd and tomato juice. Bring to the boil and then simmer until the bottle gourd is cooked. Add lemon juice and salt to taste. Reheat and serve hot, garnishing with coriander leaves. When the curry is done the fenugreek seeds will be swollen. They have a bitter taste so warn your diners. We like the bitterness but you may have to acquire the taste. However, without fenugreek *palida* is incomplete.

Chickpeas with Cheese
Channa Paneer
Serves 4—6

Gram and cheese is not a very common combination but a Punjabi friend gave me this recipe. I tried it and enjoyed it. If you can buy the tinned variety this will reduce the cooking time as they are cooked and soaked in brine. To use the tinned variety just drain them and proceed with the actual cooking.

225g (8 oz) chickpeas (kabuli channa)

250g (9 oz) paneer *(page 46)*

4 tablespoons ghee or oil

salt to taste

1 teaspoon garam masala (pages 54–6)

Ingredients to be ground together

1 large onion

4 cloves garlic

2.5-cm (1-inch) piece fresh ginger

a handful coriander leaves

1 teaspoon coriander seeds

1/2 teaspoon cumin seeds

1/2 teaspoon chilli powder

1/2 teaspoon turmeric powder

Pick and wash the chickpeas and soak them overnight or for 24 hours. Drain. Cut the *paneer* into cubes and fry until the pieces are evenly brown. Keep the fried *paneer* aside. Heat the ghee or oil in a large pan and fry the ground ingredients until the oil separates. Add the chickpeas and enough hot water to cover them. Bring to the boil, cover and simmer until the chickpeas are tender. Add salt to taste. This dish should have a thick gravy so if your gravy is too thin remove the lid during the last stages of cooking to allow any excess liquid to evaporate. Just before serving gently fold in the *paneer* and sprinkle in the garam masala. Delicious served with any of the bread dishes on pages 226–37.

Black Gram
Masala Urad
Serves 4—6

A dish we always order on our late-night outings to the *dhabas* — cafés — on the highways leading out of Hyderabad, my hometown. On my last trip the 'boss' allowed me into the kitchen to watch how it was made.

1 cup whole black gram with skin (urad)
1 tablespoon bengal gram (channa dhal*)*
1 onion, chopped
2.5-cm (1-inch) piece fresh ginger, crushed
4 green chillies, chopped
1 tomato, chopped

½ cup single cream
½ cup natural yogurt, beaten
½ teaspoon chilli powder
½ teaspoon turmeric powder
½ teaspoon cumin powder
2 tablespoons ghee or oil
salt to taste

Soak the black gram and bengal gram overnight. Next day drain the *dhals* and place them in a heavy pan. Add water to cover them and cook until they are tender. The black gram will remain whole but the bengal gram will be mushy. Gently mash with a wooden spoon. Cool the *dhals* slightly and fold in the cream and yogurt. Heat the ghee in a frying pan and fry the onion, ginger, chillies and tomato until the onion is light brown. Add the powdered spices and salt and fry until the oil separates. Add the oil and spices to the *dhals* and mix well. Simmer the *dhal* for a few minutes stirring constantly to avoid the cream and yogurt curdling. This dish can be served hot or cold with chappatis.

Mixed Pulses with Vegetables
Milee Dhal aur Sabzi
Serves 4–6

I have listed a combination of pulses for this recipe but if you do not want to buy them all try it out with the mixed pulses you can buy at health-food shops and supermarkets. The total weight should be approximately 225g (8 oz).

1 tablespoon each: whole green gram, chickpeas, black chickpeas, black-eyed beans, dried green peas, red lentils, kidney beans and bengal gram
175g (6 oz) cauliflower florets
6 shallots, peeled and left whole

4 tablespoons ghee or oil
2 onions, finely sliced
salt to taste
225g (8 oz) paneer (page 46), cubed and fried until golden brown
2 tomatoes, chopped

Ingredients to be ground to a paste
8 cloves garlic
8 large dried red chillies
1 tablespoon coriander seeds
2 teaspoons cumin seeds
1 tablespoon poppy seeds

1 tablespoon desiccated coconut
2.5-cm (1-inch) piece fresh ginger

Soak the *dhals* for 8 hours or overnight. Cook in a pressure cooker with 2 cups water. (Check the cooking time on your own pressure cooker as each one varies.) If you do not have a pressure cooker cook in an ordinary pan with 3 cups of water. First bring to the boil and then allow to simmer until the *dhals* are cooked. If the mixture is too thick add a little hot water. Add the cauliflower and shallots and mix well. Heat the ghee in a separate pan and fry the onion until golden brown. Add the ground paste and fry until the oil separates. Add salt to taste and the tomato and fry for a further 1 minute. Add everything from the frying pan to the mixed *dhals* and mix well. Simmer for a further 5 minutes. Just before serving fold in the *paneer*. Serve hot with plain boiled rice or with any of the breads on pages 226–37.

Bengal Gram with Bottle Gourd
Doodhi Channa
Serves 4–6

A very popular dish particularly favoured by the Deccan Muslims. Use either courgettes or marrow instead of bottle gourd if you prefer.

4 tablespoons ghee or oil
1 onion, finely sliced
1 teaspoon chilli powder
1 teaspoon coriander powder
½ teaspoon turmeric powder
2.5-cm (1-inch) piece fresh
   ginger, crushed
3 green chillies
2 tomatoes, chopped
225g (8 oz) bengal gram
   (channa dhal) *soaked*
   overnight

225g (8 oz) bottle gourd,
   peeled, pith and seeds
   removed and cut into bite-
   size pieces
1 teaspoon garam masala
   (pages 54–6)
juice of 1 lemon
salt to taste
a handful coriander leaves

Ingredients for final fry *(tarka)* (page 49)
4 tablespoons oil
a pinch asafoetida
2 cloves garlic, crushed
1 dried red chilli

½ teaspoon cumin seeds
½ teaspoon mustard seeds
a few curry leaves

194

Heat the ghee or oil in a large pan and fry the onion until golden brown. Reduce the heat and add chilli powder, coriander powder, turmeric powder, ginger, chillies and tomato. Fry for 5 minutes. Add the drained bengal gram and fry for 2 minutes. Add 3 cups water and bottle gourd. Cook until the bengal gram is tender but not mushy. Add garam masala, lemon juice and salt to taste. Heat the remaining oil in a frying pan and fry the *tarka* ingredients until the mustard seeds begin to crackle and the garlic is golden brown. Add the oil and spices to the *dhal* and cover the pan immediately. Serve hot, garnishing with coriander leaves with plain boiled rice or any bread preparation. You can keep this dish dry or have a little gravy.

Red Lentils with Skin
Sabit Masoor Dhal

Serves 4–6

My family love this dish, and it is prepared for lunch every Monday. When I was working in India last year my mother always set aside a bowlful for me to have when I returned home from work. I also remember with love when my *nanima* (mother's mother) was totally paralyzed yet when I visited her she tugged my nose and told me that she had saved a bowl of *masoor dhal* for me in the *pinjara* – a cupboard with mesh instead of glass to keep the food items cool and free from insects. Dear *nanima*, this recipe is in remembrance of you.

175g (6 oz) whole red lentils
  with skin (masoor)
50g (2 oz) red gram (arhar
  or tuvar dhal)
4 cups water
½ teaspoon turmeric powder
1 teaspoon cumin powder
2 teaspoons coriander
  powder

1 teaspoon chilli powder
1 onion, finely sliced
2 cloves garlic, crushed
a few curry leaves
2 tomatoes, quartered
a handful coriander leaves
salt to taste
juice of 2 lemons

Ingredients for final fry *(tarka)* (page 49)
4 tablespoons oil
1 teaspoon mustard seeds

2 cloves garlic, crushed
a few curry leaves

Wash the lentils and place them in a large heavy pan. Add the water, powdered spices, onion, garlic and curry leaves. Bring to the boil and then simmer until the lentils are soft. The red lentils will remain whole and the red gram will be mushy. Mash gently with a potato masher or a wooden spoon. Add the tomatoes, coriander leaves, salt to taste and lemon juice. In a small frying pan heat the oil and fry the *tarka* ingredients until the mustard seeds crackle. Pour the oil and spices over the *dhal* and cover the pan immediately to retain the aroma. Reheat the *dhal* and serve hot with plain rice.

Lentils with Greens
Dhal Palak
Serves 4—6

My friends Ruki, Kali and I were known as the 'Teen Devian' — three maidens of Marredpally, the elite town where we grew up in the same street. This recipe is from my Sindhi friend Ruki's home where I enjoyed several delicious meals, although she could not eat at my house as they were strict vegetarians. Kali is a Telegu Rao girl and I am a Muslim. What a combination we made.

100g (4 oz) bengal gram (channa dhal)
4 tablespoons ghee or oil
1 onion, finely sliced
2.5-cm (1-inch) piece fresh ginger, crushed
4 green chillies, chopped (seeded for a milder flavour)
½ teaspoon turmeric
½ teaspoon chilli powder

salt to taste
175g (6 oz) spinach, washed and coarsely chopped (use frozen if necessary)
100g (4 oz) fenugreek (methi bhaji) or if unavailable increase ordinary spinach to 275g (10 oz)
50g (2 oz) dill leaves
100g (4 oz) tomatoes, quartered

Pick and wash the *dhal* and soak in water for 30 minutes. Heat the oil in a large pan and fry the onion and ginger until the onion is soft. Drain the *dhal* and add to the pan with chillies, turmeric and chilli powder. Add 1 cup hot water and bring to the boil. Reduce heat and simmer the *dhal* until it is soft and mushy. Mash with a wooden spoon or potato masher until smooth. Add salt to taste. Add the remaining ingredients and simmer for 5 more minutes. Reheat fully before serving and if the consistency has become too thick add a little hot water. Delicious with any bread accompaniment and freshly made natural yogurt.

Bengal Gram with Snake Gourd
Anglo-Indian Style
Serves 4–6

My childhood was a very happy one and I grew up with some lovely friends. I had lost touch with my Anglo-Indian friend Caro but we met up last year after nearly fourteen years. She cooked this dish for me which I had eaten many times at her place when we were children. Use marrow, courgettes or pumpkin instead of snake gourd if you prefer.

175g (6 oz) bengal gram
  (channa dhal)
4 tablespoons oil
2 green chillies, left whole
1 onion, sliced
2 cloves garlic, crushed
2.5-cm (1-inch) piece fresh
  ginger, crushed
a few curry leaves

1 teaspoon chilli powder
½ teaspoon turmeric powder
salt to taste
1 medium-sized snake gourd,
  peeled, pith removed and
  cut into large pieces
2 tomatoes, quartered
a handful coriander leaves,
  chopped

Pick and wash the *dhal* and cook in 1 cup water until tender but not mushy. In a separate pan heat the oil and fry the chillies, onion, garlic, ginger, curry leaves, chilli powder, turmeric powder and salt. When the onions are soft add the snake gourd and fry for a few minutes. Add a few drops of hot water, cover the pan and allow to simmer until the snake gourd is done. Add the cooked *dhal* and mix well. Adjust salt if necessary. Add the tomatoes and reheat just before serving. Garnish with coriander leaves.

The Anglo-Indians I know eat very hot food so reduce the chilli if necessary. Another interesting point is that they tend to leave the *dhals* whole and not mashed like most other recipes.

Rice with Lentils and Lentil Soup
Masoor Chawal Sarki
Serves 4−6

This is a very popular Bhori dish which is only prepared by this community of Muslims. Bhoris are now spread all over India but their original base was Gujerat and our mother tongue is therefore Gujerati instead of Urdu.

2 cups red lentils (masoor dhal)
½ teaspoon turmeric powder
2 cups patna rice, washed and soaked for 2 hours
4 tablespoons oil
2 medium-sized onions, finely sliced and deep-fried until golden brown

2 cloves garlic, crushed
1 teaspoon cumin powder
½ teaspoon chilli powder
a handful fresh coriander leaves, chopped
salt to taste

FOR THE SOUP
1 onion, finely chopped
a handful coriander leaves, chopped

a few mint leaves
juice of 1 lemon or to taste

Ingredients to be ground to a paste
4 tablespoons desiccated coconut
2 green chillies
4 cloves garlic
3 peppercorns

1½ tablespoons poppy seeds, dry-roasted (page 48)
½ teaspoon cumin seeds
2 teaspoons almond powder
salt to taste

Boil 1 cup red lentils in 2 cups water and half the turmeric until soft and mushy. Mash with a potato masher until smooth and keep aside. Boil the second cup of red lentils in 2 cups water and then simmer until the red lentils are half done. Drain the water and reserve. Keep aside the red lentils. Cook the rice in 3 cups water until half done. Drain the water and loosen the grains. Keep aside. Heat the oil and gently fry the onions, garlic, cumin powder, chilli powder and coriander leaves. Add salt to taste. Gently fold in the drained lentils and keep aside. In a heavy pan with a tight-fitting lid place a layer of rice and a layer of lentils alternately, with a final layer of rice. Sprinkle a little water and add a few dabs of ghee or butter. Cover the pan (if necessary with a sheet of foil first) and leave to simmer on the lowest possible heat to allow the rice and lentils to fully cook. Add the reserved water and ground paste to the mashed lentils and mix well. Add salt to taste and bring to the boil. Just before serving add the chopped onion, coriander leaves and lemon juice. Serve the layered rice and *sarki* (soup) separately.

In India to enhance the taste of the *sarki* a burning ember is added to the pan which is removed just before serving.

Serve in soup plates as this dish is delicious when a lot of *sarki* has been added to the rice.

Bengal Gram Curry with Chappatis
Chakolia
Serves 4−6

A popular Deccani dish. Meat is sometimes added when the *dhal* is being cooked. If you wish you can add 100g (4 oz) big chunks of soya meat.

1 cup bengal gram (channa dhal), *picked and washed*
4−6 chappatis, a few days old, cut into small pieces
2 tablespoons ghee or oil
1 large onion, finely sliced
½ teaspoon chilli powder
1½ teaspoons coriander powder

½ teaspoon turmeric powder
½ teaspoon garlic paste (page 56)
½ teaspoon ginger paste (page 56)
salt to taste
¼ teaspoon garam masala
a few mint leaves

Soak the *dhal* and chappati pieces in separate bowls of water for 30 minutes. Fry the sliced onion until golden brown. Add the chilli powder, turmeric powder, coriander powder, garlic and ginger pastes and salt. Fry on a reduced heat for 2 minutes. Drain the *dhal* and add to the spices and mix well. Add 3 cups of water and bring to the boil. Reduce the heat and allow the *dhal* to simmer until soft and mushy. Mash with a potato masher until smooth. Drain the chappati pieces and add to the *dhal*. Reheat quickly and just before serving sprinkle with garam masala and garnish with mint leaves. Serve with a green leafy vegetable dish and onion *kachoomber* (page 252). You can prepare this dish in advance if you wish in which case you should add the chappati pieces after you have reheated the *dhal*. Cooked *dhals* tend to absorb water so adjust the consistency if you have cooked the *dhal* in advance.

Spiced Broth
Traditional Rasam
Serves 4—6

This famous south Indian broth, known to aid digestion, is true to the fables but I find it also eases coughs and colds and warms the body during the winter months. In south India this is usually the last course of a meal. You can have it on its own or with a little plain boiled rice. Serve in tiny bowls with soup spoons. I have chosen the three variations which are family favourites.

½ cup red gram (tuvar *or* arhar dhal)*, picked and washed*
4 cups water
½ teaspoon turmeric powder
1 tablespoon oil
2 cloves garlic, crushed with peel

4 tablespoons tamarind juice (page 60)
a pinch asafoetida
salt to taste
a handful fresh coriander leaves, chopped

Ingredients to be dry-roasted and ground
10 black peppercorns
1½ teaspoons cumin seeds
1 teaspoon mustard seeds

1 teaspoon coriander seeds
1 dried red chilli

Place the *dhal*, water, turmeric and oil in a heavy pan (or pressure cooker). Bring to the boil and then simmer until the *dhal* is mushy. Pass through a sieve and add more hot water if the consistency is thicker than tomato juice. Add the remaining ingredients and bring back to the boil and then simmer for 5— 7 minutes. Serve hot. My sons love this broth but I strain it for them as they do not like the whole spices. It should have a distinctive sour taste so adjust with lemon juice as necessary.

Lime Juice Broth
Nimbu Rasam
Serves 4−6

I sometimes add a piece of jaggery, the size of a walnut, to this recipe and the combination provides all the daily vitamin C and minerals required.

4 teaspoons oil
½ teaspoon mustard seeds
a pinch asafoetida
a few curry leaves
1 dried red chilli
4 cups water
juice of 2 limes or lemons
4 cloves garlic, crushed with
  peel
2.5-cm (1-inch) piece of fresh
  ginger, sliced

1 teaspoon roasted cumin
  seeds
1 teaspoon cumin powder
½ teaspoon coriander
  powder
½ teaspoon turmeric powder
salt to taste
a handful fresh coriander
  leaves, chopped

Heat the oil in a large pan and fry the mustard seeds, asafoetida, curry leaves and chilli until the mustard seeds crackle. Standing well back add the water and then the remaining ingredients. Bring to the boil and simmer for 5 minutes. Serve hot, either strained or with the herbs and spices.

Tomato Broth
Tomato Rasam
Serves 4–6

When Michael, my neighbour, had flu, this dish perked him up
and restored his appetite.

285ml (10 fl oz) tomato juice
juice of 2 lemons
110ml (4 fl oz) water
1 teaspoon oil
10 black peppercorns
1 teaspoon cumin seeds
½ teaspoon mustard seeds
a pinch asafoetida
2 whole dried chillies

a few curry leaves
½ teaspoon coriander
powder
½ teaspoon turmeric powder
2 cloves garlic crushed with
peel
salt to taste
a handful coriander leaves,
chopped

Mix the tomato juice, lemon juice and water. Heat oil in a
frying pan and on a medium heat fry all the spices and garlic.
When the mustard seeds start to crackle pour the oil and
spices over the tomato juice mixture. Bring the tomato juice
mixture to the boil. Add salt to taste and coriander leaves.
Simmer for about 5 minutes. Serve hot either strained or with
the spices and herbs. This *rasam* should have a distinctive sour
taste so adjust the quantity of lemon juice to suit your taste.

Yogurt, Egg and Cheese

Yogurt Dishes

To set yogurt at home see pages 44–5. The only days fresh yogurt is not set in my house is when we are having a Western meal and that, I am afraid, is not very often. It is therefore safe for me to say that I set yogurt nearly every day. I use it for cooking, as a salad, for sweet dishes or just to eat it on its own at the end of a meal. The nutritious values of yogurt are immense and it also has many medicinal values.

During the summer months I pick a variety of fruits and make them into jams or purées or just sugar them and freeze. In my sons' daily lunch boxes they have freshly made yogurt with either one of the homemade jams, fruit purée or thawed frozen fruits. This way they get just the natural goodness of yogurt and fruits as I never use any additives even when making jams or purées. And they love it.

Yogurt Curry with Fritters
Dahi ki Kari
Serves 4–6

A very simple yet delicious dish. Members of my family help themselves to the gravy in individual bowls, add sugar to taste and sip it like soup.

FOR THE CURRY
450g (15 oz) natural yogurt
4 tablespoons gram flour
  (besan *or* channa atta)
4 cloves garlic, ground to a
  paste
5-cm (2-inch) piece fresh
  ginger, ground to a paste
½ teaspoon chilli powder
salt to taste
½ teaspoon turmeric powder

FOR THE FRITTERS
½ cup gram flour (besan *or*
  channa atta)
1 green chilli, finely chopped
a few coriander leaves,
  chopped
salt to taste
1 tablespoon natural yogurt
a pinch baking powder

Ingredients for final fry (*tarka*) (page 49)
6 tablespoons oil
4 whole dried red chillies
1 teaspoon cumin seeds
2 cloves garlic, crushed
a few curry leaves
a pinch turmeric

Mix all the ingredients for the curry and pass through a sieve. Add 2 cups water and mix well. On a low heat cook the mixture until it becomes the consistency of thick soup. Set aside. Mix all the fritter ingredients adding a little water to make a batter of dropping consistency. Heat enough oil for deep-frying and when smoking hot drop spoonfuls of the batter. On a lower heat fry them until they are golden brown in colour. Only fry as many fritters as will comfortably fit in your frying utensil. When the fritters are golden brown drain them well and add them to the yogurt curry.

Heat 6 tablespoons oil in a small frying pan and fry the ingredients for the final fry until the whole chillies are dark in colour. Pour the oil and spices over the yogurt curry and cover the pan immediately to retain the aroma. Reheat the curry before serving.

Serve with plain boiled rice or, as we Hyderabadis do, with *moong dhal kitchdi* (page 99). Be brave and try the chillies also, as they are delicious.

Yogurt Vermicelli
Dahi Sev

Serves 4−6

This dish can be served as an accompaniment with any hot curry. Or you can serve it as a starter. It is light and will not spoil your appetite for the rest of the meal. If you have access to an Indian grocer try the Indian vermicelli which is extremely fine.

200g (7 oz) fine vermicelli
425g (15 oz) natural yogurt,
* beaten*
salt to taste
2 green chillies, finely
* chopped*
2.5-cm (1-inch) piece fresh
* ginger, crushed*

4 tablespoons oil
¼ teaspoon mustard seeds
a pinch asafoetida
a few curry leaves
1 whole dried red chilli
coriander leaves to garnish

Break the vermicelli into small pieces and boil them in salted water until soft. Drain the vermicelli well and cool. Mix vermicelli, yogurt, chillies and ginger. Add salt to taste. In a small frying pan heat the oil and fry the mustard seeds, asafoetida, curry leaves and chilli. When the mustard seeds begin to crackle pour the oil and spices over the vermicelli and fold in gently. Garnish with coriander leaves and serve cold.

Yogurt Salads
Raitha/Pachhadi
All serve 4–6

Raitha is yogurt salad which is served as an accompaniment with any hot and spicy meal. I have chosen a few variations but you can use your own ingenuity and blend in any vegetables, fruits and nuts. *Raitha* is the name used in the north of India and in the south it is called *pachhadi*.

Walnut *Raitha*

425g (15 oz) natural yogurt, beaten
1 cup shelled walnuts
6 spring onions, chopped
salt to taste
½ cucumber, shredded

Mix the yogurt, walnuts, spring onions and salt to taste. Fold in the shredded cucumber. Garnish with fresh coriander leaves if you wish or just sprinkle a pinch of paprika on the surface. Chill and serve.

Tomato and Onion *Raitha*

3 firm tomatoes, chopped
1 onion, finely chopped
425g (15 oz) natural yogurt, beaten
2 green chillies, seeded and finely chopped
¼ teaspoon sugar
a handful coriander leaves, chopped
salt and chilli powder to taste
a few mint leaves, left whole

Mix all the ingredients, except the mint leaves. Chill in the refrigerator and garnish with the mint leaves before serving.

Masala Yogurt

425g (15 oz) natural yogurt,
  beaten
2 green chillies, finely
  chopped
6 cashew nuts, coarsely
  chopped

a few mint leaves
a few coriander leaves
salt to taste

Mix all the ingredients, chill and serve.

Tarka Yogurt

425g (15 oz) natural yogurt,
  beaten

salt to taste

Ingredients for final fry *(tarka)* (page 49)
4 tablespoons oil
1 whole dried red chilli
¼ teaspoon mustard seeds
¼ teaspoon cumin seeds

a few curry leaves
a pinch asafoetida and
  turmeric powder

In a serving bowl mix the yogurt and salt and keep aside. In a small frying pan heat the oil and fry the *tarka* ingredients until the mustard seeds begin to crackle. Pour the oil and spices over the yogurt and immediately cover the bowl. Chill and serve. Just before serving fold the *tarka* ingredients into the yogurt.

Vegetable *Raitha*

Cooked and fried vegetables may be added to yogurt and made into appetizing *raithas*. I have given the recipe for potato *raitha* and alternative suggestions for other vegetables.

425g (15 oz) natural yogurt, beaten
1 large boiled potato, peeled and diced (or use sweet potato)
salt to taste
2 green chillies, finely chopped
2 tablespoons oil
¼ teaspoon mustard seeds
a few curry leaves

Mix the yogurt, potato, salt and chillies. Heat the oil in a small frying pan and fry the mustard seeds and curry leaves until the mustard seeds begin to crackle. Pour the oil and spices over the yogurt and cover the bowl. Mix well, chill and serve.

Alternative Suggestions:
1 green pepper, sliced and lightly fried in oil before mixing into the yogurt.
75g (3 oz) small okra, left whole and lightly fried in oil before mixing into the yogurt.
2 tomatoes, chopped and lightly fried, before mixing into the yogurt.
1 aubergine, sliced. Rub the slices with a little salt, turmeric powder and chilli powder to taste. Fry the aubergine slices in hot oil until they are golden brown on both sides. Drain well and fold into the yogurt.

All the above *raithas* can be garnished with fresh coriander leaves. You can use just one vegetable or combine a few and make a mixed vegetable *raitha*.

Beetroot or Carrot *Raitha*

2 cooked beetroots, diced,
  or 2 raw carrots, grated
2 green chillies, finely
  chopped
a handful coriander leaves,
  chopped
425g (15 oz) natural yogurt,
  beaten

salt to taste
4 tablespoons oil
½ teaspoon mustard seeds
a few curry leaves
1 whole dried red chilli

Mix the first five ingredients in a serving bowl and leave aside. Heat the oil in a small frying pan and fry the mustard seeds, curry leaves and chilli. When the mustard seeds begin to crackle pour the oil and the spices over the yogurt. Mix well, chill and serve.

Cauliflower Salad
Phool Gobhi Salat

100g (4 oz) tender
  cauliflower leaves and
  stems, chopped
2 green chillies, finely
  chopped
2.5-cm (1-inch) piece fresh
  ginger, crushed

2 cloves garlic, crushed
1 teaspoon cumin powder
salt to taste
425g (15 oz) natural yogurt,
  beaten

Blanch the cauliflower leaves and stems in boiling water for 2 minutes. Drain well and cool. Mix all the ingredients, chill and serve.

Egg Dishes

Eggs are packed with nutritional value and make wholesome and delicious dishes. Spiced scrambled eggs or the egg curry can be conjured up for an emergency meal and I can assure you either will be welcomed.

Eggs with Fenugreek Leaves
Anda aur Methi Bhaji

Serves 4—6

I like the combination of fenugreek leaves with eggs but if you have difficulty in getting them use ordinary chopped spinach or tender calabrese.

1 cup red lentils (masoor dhal)
225g (½ lb) fenugreek leaves
1 cup thick coconut milk (pages 58–60)
4 tablespoons oil

1 large onion, finely sliced
5 hardboiled eggs, coarsely chopped
juice of ½ a lemon
a handful coriander leaves

Ingredients to be ground to a paste (use oil or a little coconut milk to facilitate the grinding)

2 dried red chillies
1 teaspoon cumin seeds
½ teaspoon mustard seeds
4 cloves garlic
2.5-cm (1-inch) piece fresh ginger

1 teaspoon turmeric powder
4 peppercorns
salt to taste

Cook the *dhal* in 1½ cups water until tender. Mash with a potato masher until smooth. Mix in the fenugreek leaves and coconut milk and simmer for about 10 minutes. Heat the oil in a large pan and fry the onions until golden brown. Reduce the heat and add the ground ingredients and fry until the oil separates. Add the *dhal* and fenugreek leaves mixture and mix well. Simmer until the sauce is thick. Fold in the eggs and mix well. Just before serving sprinkle on the lemon juice and garnish with coriander leaves. Delicious when served hot with a bread dish.

Spiced Hardboiled Eggs
Anda Kalia

Serves 4—6

This dish can be served as a light meal with freshly made toast, chappatis or *puris*.

6 tablespoons oil
6 hardboiled eggs, halved
1 large onion, finely sliced
1 tablespoon coriander
   powder
2.5-cm (1-inch) piece fresh
   ginger, crushed
½ teaspoon turmeric powder
¼ teaspoon garam masala
salt and pepper to taste

4 curry leaves, chopped
2 green chillies, finely
   chopped
225g (8 oz) potatoes, peeled
   and diced
100g (4 oz) small frozen peas
chopped tomato and
   coriander leaves for
   garnish

Heat the oil in a non-stick wok or frying pan and fry the eggs until brown on all sides. Remove and keep aside. Reheat the oil and fry the onions until golden brown in colour. Mix the coriander powder, ginger, turmeric powder, garam masala, salt and pepper, curry leaves and chillies with a little water to make a paste. Add the paste to the browned onions and on a reduced heat fry until the water has evaporated and the oil separated. Add the potatoes and peas and sprinkle enough water to cook them in. Cover the wok or frying pan and allow to simmer until the potatoes are done. Add the eggs and mix well. Serve hot, garnishing with tomato and coriander leaves.

Spicy Scrambled Eggs
Akoori
Serves 4–6

A typically Parsi dish ideal for a Sunday breakfast. It can also be served on freshly made toast as a snack or on biscuits or bite-size pieces of toast as cocktail eats or even as a filling in vol-au-vents.

4 large eggs, beaten well
2 onions, finely chopped
a handful coriander leaves,
  chopped
2 green chillies, finely
  chopped (add more if you
  wish)

1 firm tomato, chopped
salt and pepper to taste
3 tablespoons oil or butter

Heat the oil or butter in a wok or frying pan and fry the onions until soft. Add the coriander leaves, green chillies and tomato. Stir-fry for 1 minute. Remove from the heat. Drain any excess oil. Return the wok to a low heat. Add the beaten eggs and seasoning and stir all the time until the mixture has the consistency of firm scrambled eggs. Serve hot. Alternatively, you can fry this mixture into individual omelettes and you will then have the Parsi *poro*. If you are making omelettes you can also add 1 boiled potato, peeled and diced.

Eggs on Potato Chip Sticks
Sali pur Eeda
Serves 4

Another popular Parsi dish, this features whole eggs on potato chip sticks cooked gently on a low heat or baked. (I have used the ready-made chip sticks but you can make your own in the following way. Peel 4 large potatoes and cut into julienne strips. Soak the potato strips in salted water for half an hour. Heat enough oil for deep-frying. Drain the water from the potato strips and fry in small batches. Do not stir till the potato strips reach the surface of the oil. Fry until they are golden brown and drain on kitchen paper.)

1 large packet potato chip
* sticks*
* (ready salted flavour)*

4 large eggs
salt and pepper to taste

Spread the potato chips in a large frying pan. Pour 8 tablespoons water and cook on a low heat until the water has evaporated. By the time the water evaporates the potato chips will have become soft. Gently break the eggs over the potato chips making sure they are whole. Cover the pan and cook on a low heat until the eggs are set. You can make this in one large dish or in individual servings. Serve hot, garnishing with chopped coriander leaves or grated cheese and a sprinkle of paprika.

Spiced Eggs on Buttered Toast
Pau pur Eeda
Serves 4–6

The egg mixture can also be used as a sandwich filling after it has been cooled. A wholesome snack for children after school.

3 teaspoons ghee or butter
1 onion, finely chopped
4 hardboiled eggs, coarsely
  chopped
a handful coriander leaves,
  chopped

1 green chilli, finely chopped
  (or to taste)
a pinch turmeric powder
½ teaspoon garam masala
a pinch red chilli powder
salt and pepper to taste

Heat the ghee or butter in a non-stick wok or frying pan and fry the onions until golden brown in colour. Add the eggs and the rest of the ingredients and stir-fry for a few minutes. Serve hot on buttered toast and garnish with chopped tomato.

Egg Curry Rafi Style
Andoan ka Salan
Serves 4–6

This is a favourite dish of my family especially when I serve it
as an accompaniment to *biryani* or any *pilau*.

4 tablespoons oil
1 large onion, finely chopped
2 tablespoons ground
  almonds
1 teaspoon chilli powder (or
  to taste)
1 teaspoon turmeric powder
1 teaspoon coriander powder
2 cloves garlic, crushed

2.5-cm (1-inch) piece fresh
  ginger, crushed
400g (14 oz) chopped tinned
  tomatoes
50g (2 oz) creamed coconut
2 bay leaves
salt to taste
6 eggs, hardboiled and
  halved

Heat the oil in a large pan and fry the onion until golden
brown in colour. Reduce the heat and add the almonds, chilli
powder, turmeric powder, coriander powder, garlic, ginger.
Mix well and fry until the oil separates. Add the tomatoes,
coconut, bay leaves and salt to taste. Simmer for about 20
minutes. If the sauce has become too thick add a little hot
water and adjust seasoning if necessary. Add the eggs and
gently cover them with the gravy. Simmer for about 5 minutes.
Serve hot with one of the above dishes or plain rice or
chappati.

I sometimes also add sliced green and red pepper and this
enhances the flavour. If you are adding peppers add them 5
minutes before you add the eggs as they should not be
overcooked.

217

Cheese Dishes

Most families in India make their own cheese — *paneer* (page 46). If you are not successful use feta cheese or ricotta. Any cheese eaten everyday with honey and a few almonds is one of the choicest tonics. Cheese is life-giving support to the brain and we must thank God for such a gift.

Cheese Snacks
Paneer Pakoras
Serves 4–6

A tasty light snack. Ideal for tea parties and children's parties.

225g (8 oz) paneer
½ cup plain flour, sieved
1 teaspoon salt
1 teaspoon chilli powder (or to taste)
1 teaspoon dry mango powder (amchur)
½ teaspoon omum (ajwain) seeds
oil for deep-frying

Cut the *paneer* into cubes. Mix the flour, salt, chilli powder, dry mango powder and omum seeds with a little water to make a batter of dropping consistency. Heat the oil in a *karai* or wok. Dip the *paneer* cubes in the batter and when the oil is nearly smoking drop in a few at a time and fry until the cubes are golden brown on all sides. Serve hot with tomato ketchup.

Cheese Dip
Serves 4–6

Delicious with *samosas* and fritters. I normally serve this with raw vegetables like carrot, cauliflower, celery, cucumber and mushrooms, but at a large party I served this and all my guests were dipping their *samosas* and fritters in it and thoroughly enjoying it. So instead of serving the traditional chutneys try this as a sauce. The recipe is another of my own innovations.

100g (4 oz) soft full-cream cheese
150ml (5 fl oz) sour cream or natural yogurt
2 cloves garlic, crushed finely
salt and pepper to taste
a few mint leaves, finely chopped
a few coriander leaves, finely chopped
1 green chilli, seeded and finely chopped
a pinch chilli powder or paprika

With an electric hand whisk mix the cheese, sour cream, garlic, salt and pepper until you have a creamy texture. Fold in the herbs and put in a serving bowl. Sprinkle with chilli powder or paprika. Chill and serve.

The taste of garlic is prominent in this sauce but you can reduce the quantity to suit your taste. If your dip is too thick you can thin it by adding a few drops of milk and lemon juice.

Cottage Cheese with Tomato Sauce
Paneer Peshawari
Serves 4–6

The Peshawari people are originally mountain people, strong, big and healthy. I returned to Madras to visit my old boarding school and after twenty-one years I was delighted to find the *peshawari choukidar* (guard) was still on duty. He had often helped me when I used to sneak out to meet my boyfriend, now my husband. We exchanged lovely memories and he gave me his wife's recipe of this delicious dish which she used to make for some of the boarders on festive occasions. Instead of the traditional *paneer* I have used cottage cheese and this makes an excellent substitute.

250g (9 oz) cottage cheese
250g (9 oz) very ripe
  tomatoes
5-cm (2-inch) piece fresh
  ginger, crushed
50g (2 oz) blanched almonds
50g (2 oz) cashew nuts
2½ tablespoons tomato
  ketchup

1 teaspoon chilli powder
1 teaspoon sugar
salt to taste
2 tablespoons ghee or butter
2 green chillies, finely
  chopped
a few coriander leaves,
  chopped

Put the cottage cheese in a fine sieve to drain off any excess liquid. When drained place the cottage cheese in the centre of a shallow serving dish. Chop the tomatoes. In a heavy pan cook the tomatoes and ginger with a little water for about 20 minutes. Pass through a sieve to make a tomato purée and keep aside. Heat the ghee or butter and on a low heat sauté the almonds and cashew nuts until golden brown. Add the tomato purée, tomato ketchup, chilli powder, sugar and salt to taste. Simmer until the sauce has a thick consistency, stirring often. Pour the sauce around the cheese and garnish with the green chillies and coriander leaves.

To accompany this dish we were sent light freshly baked *tandoor rotis*. You can serve hot wholemeal pitta bread. To heat pitta bread make a slit in each and place a few dabs of butter. Then wet the bread, cover in foil and heat in a hot oven for about 10 minutes.

Cheese Ball Curry
Paneer Kofta
Serves 4—6

A simply delicious curry when served with *bagara chawal* or *puris*.

300g (11 oz) potatoes, boiled, peeled and mashed
100g (4 oz) paneer
25g (1 oz) cornflour
salt and pepper to taste
a few coriander leaves, chopped

oil for deep-frying
4 tablespoons ghee or butter
100g (4 oz) single cream
1 tablespoon tomato purée
1 teaspoon chilli powder
salt to taste

Ingredients to be dry-roasted and ground
1 large onion
2 tablespoons desiccated coconut
7 cloves garlic
2.5-cm (1-inch) piece fresh ginger

2 green chillies
2 dry red chillies
2 teaspoons coriander seeds
1 teaspoon cumin seeds
2 tablespoons almonds
2 teaspoons poppy seeds

Knead together the first five ingredients. Make small balls. Heat the oil in a *karai* or wok and when nearly smoking drop in a few cheese balls at a time and fry until they are evenly golden in colour. Drain and keep warm. Heat the ghee in a *karai* or wok and fry the ground ingredients until the oil separates. Reduce the heat and gradually stir in the cream. Mix well and allow to simmer for 2 minutes. Add the tomato purée, chilli powder and salt to taste and continue to simmer for another 5 minutes. Add the *paneer koftas* and cover them with sauce or place on a serving dish and pour the sauce over them. Garnish with coriander leaves and almond flakes if you wish.

Cheese and Spinach
Paneer Palak
Serves 4–6

Paneer and spinach make a wonderful combination. I have used very few spices as I like to retain the natural taste of spinach.

225g (8 oz) paneer, cubed
oil for deep-frying
1 large onion, coarsely
  chopped
2.5-cm (1-inch) piece fresh
  ginger, crushed (or ½
  teaspoon ginger paste,
  page 56)

3 green chillies, seeded and
  chopped
½ teaspoon turmeric powder
salt to taste
225g (8 oz) chopped frozen
  spinach, thawed and excess
  water drained

Heat enough oil for deep-frying and fry the *paneer* cubes until golden brown. Drain and keep warm. Remove excess oil leaving 2 tablespoons. Reheat the oil and fry the onions, ginger, chillies, turmeric powder and salt until the onions are slightly soft. Add the spinach and simmer for 2 or 3 minutes. Fold in the *paneer* cubes. Serve hot with any bread preparation.

Spiced Cheese
Paneer Masala
Serves 4—6

This is a Rajasthani dish. When I was touring Rajasthan I tried new dishes daily but found I was always including this as I really loved it. *Paneer* has a very bland taste, so I have used quite a lot of chillies, but you can reduce the chilli quantities to suit your taste. Serve with any bread preparation.

350g (12 oz) paneer, *cubed*
oil for deep-frying
2 tomatoes, chopped
salt to taste

½ cup single cream
1 teaspoon chilli sauce
  (see page 242)
3 tablespoons oil

Ingredients to be individually dry-roasted and then ground to a paste

1 medium-sized onion,
  chopped
1 tablespoon poppy seeds
1 tablespoon desiccated
  coconut
5-cm (2-inch) cinnamon
  quill
2 cloves

10 peppercorns
6 large dried red chillies
3 teaspoons coriander seeds
1½ teaspoons cumin seeds
5 cloves garlic
2.5-cm (1-inch) piece fresh
  ginger

Heat enough oil in a *karai* or wok. When hot fry the *paneer* cubes until golden brown on all sides. Drain and keep warm. Remove any excess oil leaving 3 tablespoons in the *karai* or wok. Reheat the oil on a medium heat and fry the ground paste until the raw smell disappears. Add the tomatoes and salt and fry for 2 minutes. Reduce heat to the lowest setting and gradually add the cream, stirring constantly to avoid curdling.

Add the chilli sauce and *paneer* cubes. Stir gently to cover the *paneer* with the sauce. (If the sauce is very thick add a few drops of hot water.) Simmer for 10 minutes. Serve hot, garnishing with coriander leaves and lemon wedges if you wish.

Seasoned Cheese
Paneer Bhoorji
Serves 4—6

You can use ordinary cottage cheese for this dish. Drain some of the excess fluid before you proceed.

2 tablespoons ghee or oil
1 small onion, finely chopped
350g (12 oz) paneer,
   crumbled
¼ teaspoon turmeric powder
salt and pepper to taste

2.5-cm (1-inch) piece fresh
   ginger, crushed
2 green chillies, finely
   chopped
a few coriander leaves to
   garnish

Heat the ghee or oil in a *karai* or wok and fry the onion until golden brown. Add *paneer*, turmeric powder, salt and pepper. Stir-fry for 3 minutes. Stir in the ginger and green chillies. Serve hot or cold garnished with coriander leaves. Serve a tossed salad and fresh toast as accompaniments.

Breads

Breads are popular as the staple foods in the north of India whereas in the south it is mainly rice. We have such a wide variety besides chappatis which are prepared daily in most homes for all the three main meals. I have chosen eight recipes and any of these can be served as an accompaniment with curries.

We generally use *atta* or chappati flour which is available from Indian grocers. Try both the refined and the coarser variety and then decide which you prefer. If you do not have access to an Indian grocer use wholemeal flour which you can purchase from supermarkets and health-food shops.

Many of the breads freeze well and I have given useful hints in the following pages. In India, of course, they are always prepared while the meal is in progress and the cook will only stop sending out hot breads when word is sent to her that no more can be consumed.

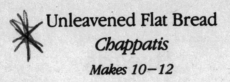

Unleavened Flat Bread
Chappatis
Makes 10–12

I was taught how to make chappatis by my *mamiji* — my mother's sister-in-law — at whose house I stayed for a while. My family was trying to dissuade me from marrying John (my Malaysian husband), and my *mamiji* was doing her best to teach me some of the domestic arts to help me find a nice Bhori husband. I remember how she scolded me when I could not make a perfectly round chappati and used to smack my knuckles with the rolling pin. She used to say she wanted the chappatis as round as the world and not in different shapes of its continents!

When I was only about five years old I used to watch my grandmother make chappatis and she always gave me one fresh off the *tava* and smeared it with ghee and sprinkled sugar. She then rolled it for my tiny hands and told me to hide and eat it as my mother did not approve of eating between meals.

I use my fingers to lift off the chappatis from the hot *tava* but I have suggested you use a flat spatula just to ensure you do not burn your fingers. I have also suggested you roll out all the chappatis first although we Indians roll one out while another is being roasted so that the chappatis reach the table really fresh and piping hot. You will be able to use your fingers and formulate a rhythm to roll and roast after a few attempts.

250g (9 oz) wheatflour (atta)
or wholemeal flour
½ teaspoon salt

2 tablespoons ghee or butter
tepid water
a little dry flour

Sieve the flour and salt in a large mixing bowl. Make a well and add enough water to make a soft pliable dough. The amount of water used will depend on the type and grade of the flour you are using, the atmosphere of your kitchen and also the heat of

the oil is piping hot or they will become greasy and will not fully puff out. I use chopsticks to turn them over and remove them when fried but I suggest you use two flat wooden spatulas or slotted spoons. Using two spatulas will prevent any hot oil splashing when turning over the *puris* and will also make them easier to hold while you drain off excess oil. When I am making *puris* my older son helps me knead the dough balls, I roll them out and my husband does the frying. My young son keeps count. I normally prepare four per person but you can adjust this to suit your appetites.

250g (9 oz) wheatflour (atta) ·	*tepid water*
or wholemeal flour or	*a little dry flour for dusting*
strong plain flour	*while rolling*
½ teaspoon salt	*oil for deep-frying*
2 tablespoons oil	

Before I start preparing the *puris* I do two things. First I flour a working surface on which I place the rolled-out *puris* and then I line a wicker basket or a large colander with kitchen paper to hold the *puris* when they are fried.

Sieve the flour and salt in a large mixing bowl. Make a well and add the oil. Using your fingers gently mix to get a slightly crumbly texture. Very gradually add water to bind the flour into a smooth but firm dough. Cover the dough with a bowl or cling film and leave to rest for about 30 minutes.

Knead the dough again for about 5 minutes using your knuckles and then divide it into equal portions. Take one portion (keeping the others covered) and roll it between your palms to make a smooth ball. Flatten it slightly and then roll it out on a lightly floured board into thin rounds about 10cm (4 inches) in diameter. Place it on the floured working surface and cover it. Roll out the remaining *puris* in the same manner. Heat enough oil in a *karai* or wok or a chip pan until it is nearly smoking. Lift the *puri* you rolled out first and dust off any dry flour. Gently slide it into the hot oil to prevent any splashes. At first the *puri* will sink but within seconds it will rise to the top of the oil. Using the spatulas or slotted spoons gently tap the edges to encourage it to puff out. When the first side is golden brown turn it over. When the second side is the same colour lift it out of the oil and hold it for a few seconds to drain off the excess oil. Place it standing up in the prepared basket or colander as this will help to drain the oil fully. Cover the basket or colander with a kitchen towel. Fry the remaining *puris* in the same manner. Serve them immediately. If this is not possible work out your schedule so that you do not allow prepared *puris* to stand any longer than necessary. Keep them wrapped in a sheet of foil or a warmed kitchen towel if you are serving them more than 10 minutes after they have been fried.

Puris can be fried in an electric fryer or an ordinary chip pan. This might be best for those attempting *puris* for the first time to avoid any accidents. If you are using a traditional wok and working with two spatulas make sure your wok is sitting firmly on the ring and that there is no chance of it tipping over.

The Bengalis roll out their *puris* (or *luchis*, as they call them) on greased boards to prevent them sticking. The advantage of this is that you will have no burnt sediment in the oil. The oil should be thoroughly cooled and sieved before bottling for use again. If I have used dry flour to help me during the rolling I cool the oil and then sieve it through a *chinois* — a cone-shaped sieve. If you use this you can strain the oil directly into the bottle.

Puris cannot be frozen but if you have any leftovers crumble them in a dish and cover them with cream and the jam of your choice. Toss it and eat it as a snack. I always try and have one or two left over for this reason.

Puris made from plain flour are also a favourite with Muslims and they are served with our style of rice pudding (page 259).

Unleavened Layered Bread
Parathas
Makes 12

When you study this recipe your first thought will be that it is too hard and complicated. Yet many of you make puff pastry and this is basically the same method. Making *parathas* should be easier as you are working with small portions of dough which makes it easier to handle. When I attended the Culinary Techniques Course at Robert Carrier's school I made a hopeless mess preparing puff pastry yet when I demonstrated *parathas* to my Swedish teacher he was very pleased. In India *parathas* are made into round, square or triangular shapes. My recipe gives you triangular shapes and hints to make the other two shapes. However, if you acquire other shapes do not worry too much as they will still taste the same and after a few attempts you will obtain one of our traditional shapes. Remember, 'practice makes perfect'.

I love eating hot *parathas* with soft full cream cheese sprinkled with salt, pepper and chilli powder. At any rate *parathas* are very rich as they are smeared with ghee between the layers. Two are sufficient per person but there are some people who can consume more. This does not prove that they are greedy as these are really delicious. No one dining in my house has managed to refuse them because they are worried about the calories. I usually say, 'Eat them today and cut down your calorie intake tomorrow.' Traditionally *parathas* are made with wheatflour but I like combining a little plain flour as this improves the texture. They can also be made with strong plain flour, giving a heavier and rubbery texture.

225g (8 oz) wheatflour
  (atta) or wholemeal flour
100g (4 oz) plain flour
½ teaspoon salt
150g (5 oz) melted ghee or
  clarified butter (you may
  not use it all)

water
a little dry flour for dusting

Sieve the flours with salt in a large mixing bowl. Make a well and pour in one teaspoon of the melted ghee or butter. Using your fingers rub the ghee into the flour so that you have a crumbly texture. Make a well again and, gradually adding water, make a soft but pliable dough. Wrap in cling film and keep aside for at least half an hour. Knead the dough again for about 10 minutes and divide it into 12 equal portions and keep them covered.

Now, unlike the chappatis and *puris*, these cannot all be rolled out first and then roasted so you have to work systematically. Collect all the items you will require: a board, rolling pin, dry flour, *tava* or a cast-iron griddle, a flat spatula and a dish lined with a kitchen towel or foil in which to stack your *parathas*.

First place the *tava* or griddle on a medium-high heat and allow it to get fairly hot. While the *tava* is getting hot take one portion of the dough and rub it between your palms to make a smooth ball. Roll it in the dry flour and flatten it slightly. Place it on a lightly floured board and roll it out to about 14cm (5½ inches) round. Grease the surface generously with ghee or butter and fold it in half. Grease the top again with ghee or butter and fold in a quarter. Roll it out again, dusting with dry flour if necessary, keeping the triangular shape. Roll it out until each side of the triangle measures about 18cm (7 inches).

By now your *tava* or griddle should have reached the required temperature. Brush it with a little ghee or butter and if it starts to smoke your *tava* or griddle is ready. Pick up the *paratha* and dust off any dry flour. Place it on the *tava* or griddle and brush it with a little ghee or butter. Cook the first side for about 1 minute. Lift it with the help of a flat spatula (I use my fingers) and turn it over to cook the other side. Sprinkle a few drops of ghee or butter along the edges of the *paratha*. If your flame is not even or the level of your floor uneven, like mine, your *tava* will heat unevenly. In this case move the *paratha* gently so it is browned evenly. Place the roasted *paratha* on the kitchen towel or foil and brush it with a little more ghee or butter. Wrap it to keep warm while you are preparing the remaining *parathas*.

To achieve the square shape, grease the first round and then fold in the four edges, greasing each fold until you have a square shape. Roll it, retaining the square shape, until each side of the square is about 18cm (7 inches) long.

To achieve the round shape grease the first round and make a cut with a knife from the centre outwards. Using this cut roll it into a cone shape and then squash it in from the broad top to the tip. If you have a naughty tip sticking out tuck it in. Roll out on a floured board until it is 18cm (7 inches) in diameter.

Parathas can also be made with strong plain flour following the same method but these will have a heavier and rubbery texture.

Cooled *parathas* can be stacked in a foil sheet, packed and then frozen. To reheat place the packet in a moderate oven and heat for about 20−25 minutes or grease a hot *tava* or griddle and reheat each *paratha* individually after thawing them for about ½ minute on each side. They can also be heated in the microwave oven, but remember to remove the foil. One thawed *paratha* will only require 30 seconds on full setting.

Layered Bread with Stuffing
Bhare Huvey Paratha

Makes 4−6

The most common varieties of stuffed *parathas* are those with a potato, pea, cauliflower or lentil filling. I tried this recipe with spinach, an idea which came to me from a wonderful Sindhi spinach dish. Sindhis originally lived in the part of India that, since 1947, has been West Pakistan. They speak their own dialect which is a strange mixture of Hindi, Gujerati and Bengali.

100g (4 oz) wheatflour (atta)
  or wholemeal flour
100g (4 oz) plain flour
½ teaspoon salt
2 tablespoons red gram
  (tuvar or arhar dhal)
¼ cup water
½ teaspoon turmeric

2.5-cm (1-inch) piece fresh
  ginger
a few coriander leaves
1 green chilli, chopped
¼ teaspoon cumin powder
salt to taste
100g (4 oz) frozen chopped
  spinach, thawed

Sieve the two flours and salt in a large mixing bowl and keep aside. In a pan add the remaining ingredients except the spinach. Bring to the boil and then simmer until the *dhal* is soft. Mash it with a potato masher and then add the spinach and mix well. Leave to simmer for 2 or 3 more minutes. Remove and allow to cool. There should be sufficient liquid to allow you to add the flours and then knead it to a soft dough. Divide the dough into equal portions and roll them out into rounds about 18cm (7 inches) in diameter dusting with dry flour if necessary. Heat a *tava* or griddle and when piping hot bake each *paratha* for 1 minute on each side. Brush with ghee and serve hot.

The Sindhis love homemade butter which they churn out of buttermilk and this is an excellent combination with spinach. I have tried it with cottage cheese and soft full cream cheese and this made a hearty and nutritious meal.

Freeze and use like ordinary *parathas*, pages 231–3.

Leavened Bread
Nan
Makes 6

Nans are traditionally baked in a tandoor oven. I know the aroma of the clay is what makes a *nan* really good but baking them in an oven is a good substitute. Habitat, for example, sell a tandoor oven and although I do not have one myself I think they would be suitable for family cooking. I usually make my *nans* in my friend's Victorian bread oven. Ready-made *nans* are available from Indian and Greek grocers. To heat them wrap them in a sheet of foil and place the packet in a hot oven for about 10 minutes.

4 cups plain flour
1 tablespoon sugar
1 teaspoon baking powder
½ teaspoon baking soda
½ teaspoon salt
2 eggs

1 cup milk
4 tablespoons natural yogurt
6 teaspoons ghee
poppy, sesame or onion seeds
   (kalonji) – optional

Sieve the flour, sugar, baking powder, soda and salt in a large mixing bowl. Make a well and add the eggs, milk, yogurt and ghee and mix well. Knead to make a soft dough. Cover and leave aside for 4–6 hours or longer if possible in a warm place. Preheat the oven to a moderate temperature. Divide the dough into 6 portions and roll them out to about 14cm (5½ inches) in diameter (In India *nans* are made into oval shapes). Place the *nans* on a lightly greased baking tray, brush them with milk and sprinkle with seeds. Bake them for about 10 minutes and serve hot. If you cannot serve immediately, keep them covered in a cloth and leave in a warm place (for example, the oven when it has cooled down slightly). *Nans* baked in a tandoor have brown spots on them. To obtain these you can remove them from the oven and place them under a hot grill for a few minutes.

Rich Chappatis
Roath
Makes 10

On the ninth and tenth days of Mohurram, the final days of the Jehad — holy war — the Shia Muslims prepare these and after prayers eat them in the names of Imam Hussain and Hassan, the grandsons of Mohammed the Prophet (Peace be on Him). The Shia Bhori Muslims also make these chappatis for weddings. The day before the wedding seven unmarried girls, one widow and one baby girl are gathered. Prayers are said for the bride and after tasting salt and a little jaggery with ghee 21 small chappatis are prepared and given to the bride. She must finish all the chappatis before leaving the room. The chappatis are the size of a five-pence piece. It's the number twenty-one which is significant as the Shia's believe in twenty-one Imams.

450g (1 lb) wheatflour (atta)
or wholemeal flour
375g (13 oz) sugar
100g (4 oz) chopped almonds
100g (4 oz) sesame seeds
100g (4 oz) chopped cashew nuts
100g (4 oz) raisins
melted ghee

Sieve the flour and add the sugar, almonds, sesame seeds, cashew nuts and raisins. Mix well so all the ingredients are well distributed. Gradually add melted ghee and make a firm dough. Cover and leave for 4–6 hours. Knead the dough again for about 5 minutes and then divide it into 10 equal portions. Heat a *tava* or griddle on medium heat until hot. Take one portion of the dough and with your hands make it into a thick round about 14cm (5½ inches) in diameter. Roast the chappatis on the *tava* until evenly brown on both sides. Serve hot.

Sliced Bread and Plain Flour Rotis
Bhaturas
Serves 4—6

2½ cups plain flour
½ teaspoon baking powder
½ teaspoon salt
6 slices bread, crumbled

110ml (4 fl oz) natural
* yogurt, beaten*
oil for deep-frying

Sieve the flour, baking powder and salt in a large mixing bowl. Add the crumbled bread and mix well. Add the yogurt and make a smooth dough (adding a little water if necessary). Cover with a damp cloth and allow to rest for 12 hours or overnight. Knead the dough again and if it sticks to your hands dust them with a little dry flour and knead again. Divide the dough into balls, the size of a walnut. Roll out each ball on a floured board to 12cm (5 inches) in diameter. Heat oil for deep-frying in a *karai* or a wok and fry the *bhaturas* until golden brown on both sides. Serve hot. To keep them warm wrap them in a kitchen towel. Delicious when served with *kabuli channa* (page 176).

Chutneys, Pickles, Preserves and Other Accompaniments

Indian chutneys and pickles are rich and varied and will stimulate even the most jaded palates (like jewellery dressing up the plainest dress). Meals are highlighted by these piquant, tantalizing and appetizing recipes. Ready-made chutneys and pickles are now widely stocked by Indian grocers, and supermarkets also offer a range. Chutneys are prepared daily in Indian homes and most of them have to be eaten within a day or a limited period, unlike pickles which mature over years.

In India rules are still adhered to when making and serving pickles (page 41). There we are blessed with strong sunshine which is ideal for pickle-making but I have learned a few 'tricks of the trade' by closely scrutinizing my house and equipment. For example, I have found the warmth coming out of the vent behind a refrigerator provides a suitable place to keep pickle jars while they are maturing. The airing cupboard and central heating boilers are also ideal places. Of course, when the sun does shine pickle jars placed on windowsills mature faster than placing them outside in the sun. The window pane acts as a reflector and although the sun may be shining brightly there is often a cool breeze outside.

Selecting chutneys and pickles for this chapter took a long time as I had more than five hundred chutneys and pickles to choose from. In the end I chose those which I felt will be most suitable in the West. I have also included a chilli sauce (the Malaysian side of me) as this is delicious served with snacks. All the chutneys and pickles I have chosen are prepared throughout India and are not native to any one state.

The West is used to traditional preserves, jams and jellies made from strawberries, raspberries, apricots, and so on. Try some of ours – ginger *murrabba*, green tomato jam, mango jam, guava jelly, banana marmalade, to mention just a few.

238

Banana Chutney
Moaz Chutney

A delicious combination of banana, dates and coconut. This chutney has a sweet-sour taste.

6 dried dates, stoned
3 ripe bananas
100g (4 oz) desiccated
  coconut
100g (4 oz) onion, chopped

a few mint leaves
2 green chillies, seeded for
  milder flavour
a pinch mustard powder
juice of ½ a lemon

Soak the dates in a little boiling water until soft. Peel the bananas. Grind all the ingredients to a fine paste. Serve.

Coriander Chutney
Dhaniya Chutney

Delicious with snacks and in sandwiches. You can also freeze it in ice-cube trays and use a cube to add extra zest to any curry with gravy.

1 bunch coriander leaves
  and tender stalks
½ coconut, grated (fresh or
  desiccated)
6 green chillies (increase or
  reduce to suit your taste)
2.5-cm (1-inch) piece fresh
  ginger

2 cloves garlic
15 raw peanuts, peeled
salt and sugar to taste
1 small raw mango, peeled
  and stone removed or juice
  of 1 lemon
a pinch sugar

Wash the coriander leaves and stalks and drain well. In an electric blender grind the coriander leaves and stalks, coconut, chillies, ginger, garlic, peanuts and salt. Use a little oil to facilitate the blending if necessary or use the lemon juice. If mango is being used grind it with the remaining ingredients. Place the chutney in a serving dish and mix in the sugar. Keep in a cool place until needed.

Mango Chutney
Aamb Chutney

I am afraid only those with access to an Indian grocer will be able to enjoy this delicious chutney. Serve with any dishes. Also try it in a cheese sandwich.

36 green mangoes
sugar (see below)
450g (1 lb) raisins
100g (4 oz) fresh ginger, cut into thin strips
20 cloves garlic, cut into thin strips or coarsely ground

15 cloves
4 cinnamon quills
100g (4 oz) chilli powder (reduce to taste)
2 cups vinegar
50g (2 oz) salt

Wash the mangoes, peel them and remove any stones. Shred the mango flesh. Apply salt liberally and store in a sterilized jar for 24 hours. Next morning put it through a sieve and remove all the water. Weigh the mango pulp and weigh out the same amount of sugar. Place the sugar in a heavy pan and add the remaining ingredients except the mangoes. Simmer over a low heat until the sugar dissolves. Add the mangoes and keep cooking gently until the chutney thickens and no moisture remains. Cool thoroughly and store in sterilized bottles. When serving ensure that your spoon is clean and dry. This will prolong the life of the chutney.

Garlic Chutney
Lasan Chi Chutney

This chutney can be kept in the refrigerator for a week. Delicious with *vangi bhath* (page 104) and *amti* (page 177). Also try it in plain scrambled eggs or omelettes.

6 tablespoons desiccated
  coconut
20 cloves garlic, peeled
2 teaspoons chilli powder (or
  to taste)

½ teaspoon turmeric powder
salt to taste
juice of 1 lemon
2 teaspoons sesame oil
1 teaspoon sugar

Grind all the ingredients together to a smooth paste.

To pep-up flagging appetites in cold weather try these 'short-term' chutneys and relishes. They require very little preparation and can be whipped up at the last minute.

Hot Lime Chutney
Nimbu Chutney

This chutney is hot but for a milder flavour remove the chilli seeds.

6 lemons
5-cm (2-inch) piece fresh
  ginger

15 dried red chillies
3 tablespoons sugar
salt to taste

Remove the juice from the lemons and grate half a lemon rind. Keep aside. Grind the ginger and chillies to a smooth paste. Add the lemon juice, rind, sugar and salt. Mix well and serve. Excellent with *biryani* and *pilaus*. This chutney will store for a fortnight in a refrigerator.

Coconut Chutney
Nariyal Chutney

This south Indian chutney is always served with *dosai* (page 68) and *idlis* (page 69).

2 tablespoons sesame oil
½ teaspoon mustard seeds
1 tablespoon bengal gram
  (channa dhal*)*
2.5-cm (1-inch) fresh ginger,
  crushed
8 green chillies, seeded for a
  milder flavour

100g (4 oz) grated coconut,
  fresh or desiccated
4 tablespoons tamarind juice
  (page 60)
salt to taste

Heat the oil in a heavy pan and fry the mustard seeds. When they start to crackle add the gram and fry until they are red in colour. Reduce the heat and add the ginger and chillies. Fry for 1 minute. Add the grated coconut and cook the mixture until it is dry. Remove from the heat and grind to a very fine paste with tamarind juice and salt. If you think the chutney needs thinning, add a little water or buttermilk.

Chilli Sauce

It is so easy to make this lovely sauce it will also save you a lot of money. I have given the quantities which will make about one bottle.

6 cloves garlic
1 thumb-size piece fresh
  ginger
6 fresh red chillies
salt to taste

2 teaspoons sugar
¼ teaspoon turmeric powder
½ cup vinegar
½ cup oil

Grind together garlic, ginger, chillies, salt, sugar and turmeric powder in a blender. Heat the oil and fry the ground ingredients for 2−3 minutes. Add the vinegar and bring to the boil. Cool thoroughly and store in airtight jars. This sauce stores indefinitely.

Aubergine Pickle
Baingan Achar

4 dark purple aubergines
1 teaspoon turmeric powder
4 tablespoons salt
4 dried red chillies
2 teaspoons mustard seeds
2 teaspoons coriander seeds
1 teaspoon cumin seeds
5-cm (2-inch) piece fresh ginger

4 cloves garlic
300ml (½ pint) vinegar
75ml (3 fl oz) oil (use mustard oil if available)
100g (4 oz) whole green chillies
1 cinnamon quill
a few curry leaves
½ cup sugar

Wash and cut the aubergines lengthwise into small pieces. Rub them over with turmeric powder and salt and set aside. Grind the chillies, mustard, coriander and cumin seeds, ginger and garlic using a little vinegar to facilitate the grinding. In a large pan heat the oil and fry the aubergines and green chillies for about 10 minutes on a medium heat. Remove to a large sterilized bowl. Reheat the oil and fry the ground paste for 5 minutes. Add the vinegar, cinnamon, curry leaves and sugar and cook until the sugar has dissolved. Remove from the heat and fold the spices into the aubergines and chillies. Allow the pickle to cool before bottling. To prolong the life of this pickle make sure that there is oil floating above the aubergines and chillies and when serving use a clean dry spoon.

Chilli Pickle
Mirch ka Achar

Each summer I grow my own chillies and the yield sees me through the whole year. I freeze most of the chillies (page 30), but some I make into a chilli sauce (page 242), or preserve whole in vinegar, salt and sugar, or use them to make this titillating pickle.

50g (2 oz) mustard seeds	*50g (2 oz) garlic cloves,*
50g (2 oz) cumin seeds	*peeled and left whole*
25g (1 oz) turmeric powder	*75g (3 oz) sugar*
50g (2 oz) garlic cloves	*2 teaspoons salt*
150ml (5 fl oz) vinegar	*450g (1 lb) green chillies,*
150ml (5 fl oz) oil (use	*washed, dried and left*
mustard oil if available)	*whole*

Grind the mustard seeds, cumin seeds, turmeric powder and garlic cloves using the vinegar to facilitate the grinding. Heat the oil in a large heavy pan and fry the ground paste for about 5 minutes on a medium heat. (If you are using mustard oil keep a window open as it tends to irritate the eyes.) Add the remaining ingredients and bring to the boil. Cook until the chillies are tender. This will take about 30 minutes. Cool thoroughly and bottle.

Hot Lime Pickle
Nimbu Achar

A good lime pickle is not only delicious with any meal but it also increases the appetite and aids digestion. Limes are now readily available even from supermarkets, but if you are unable to obtain them use ordinary lemons, choosing those with thin peels.

25 limes
225g (8 oz) salt
50g (2 oz) fenugreek seeds
50g (2 oz) mustard seeds
125g (5 oz) chilli powder

15g (½ oz) turmeric powder
600ml (1 pint) oil (mustard oil if available)
1 teaspoon asafoetida powder

Cut each lime into 8 pieces and remove the pips if you wish. Place the limes in a large sterilized jar or glass bowl. Cover them with salt and leave aside. Dry-roast the fenugreek and mustard seeds and then grind them to a fine powder. Add the ground powder, chilli powder and turmeric powder to the limes and mix well. Heat the oil until it smokes and fry the asafoetida for 1 minute. Pour the oil over the limes. Cover the jar or bowl with a heavy cloth and leave in a sunny place or a warm place like an airing cupboard for about 1 week. The limes are ready when they have become a dull brown colour and are soft. It may be necessary to leave the pickle for more than a week depending on the temperature.

Sweet Lime Pickle
Mitha Nimbu Achar

This is my favourite. Delicious with anything. You can use lemons instead of limes: each time you use a lemon do not throw the peel away. Store it in a jar with salt and when it has become soft you can make it into this simple pickle.

10 limes
5 teaspoons salt
5 teaspoons chilli powder (or
reduce if you want a
sweeter pickle)

1 cup soft brown sugar

Cut the limes into 8 pieces and cover them with salt. Leave them in a jar or glass bowl in a warm place until the peels are tender and the limes are a dull brown colour. (This will take a week or two.) Add the sugar and chilli powder and mix well with a clean wooden spoon. Leave to rest again until the sugar has dissolved and you have a nice mixture. I have not used oil or vinegar in this pickle but I have known it to keep for more than a year. If you are preparing it in a bowl transfer the pickle into jars when ready.

Mango Pickle
Aamb ka Achar

There are far too many mango pickles — the Gujerati style, Punjabi, Marwari, Andhra; in fact each family can boast its own variety. So I have decided to compromise. I tested a few variations and decided on this one which is a combination of a few styles.

Ready-made pickle masala is available from Indian grocers. You can use this powder and follow the instructions on the packet.

15 medium-sized firm green mangoes
225g (8 oz) salt
100g (4 oz) chilli powder (or more if you like your pickle really hot)
2 tablespoons turmeric powder

3 tablespoons mustard seeds
150g (5 oz) fennel seeds (sonf)
1 teaspoon asafoetida
600ml (1 pint) mustard or sesame oil

Cut the mangoes into small pieces with the seed and discard the kernel. Place in a large sterilized jar or bowl and cover with salt, chilli and turmeric powder. Mix well with a clean wooden spoon. Cover the jar or bowl with a heavy cloth and leave in a warm place for 24 hours. Dry-roast the mustard seeds and half the fennel seeds and grind to a fine powder. Heat the oil in a heavy pan and when smoking quickly fry the mustard and fennel powder and asafoetida. Remove from the heat and cool. When cool add the oil on the mangoes and the remaining fennel seeds. Mix well again. Cover and store in a warm place for about 20 days. Depending on the warmth this pickle should be ready in about 20 days or may take longer. When ready transfer into small jars so you do not handle the entire quantity each time you are serving. This pickle stores for years and matures with time.

In India newly pregnant girls always crave pickles. When a girl is caught eating pickles in secret the family knows that a happy event is ahead.

Hot Mixed Vegetable Pickle
Sabzi ka Achar

This pickle can be made with a variety of vegetables. I have suggested a few but you could also try combining kholrabi, bamboo shoots, white radish, aubergines, peppers, peas, beans, for example.

*2 large carrots, cut into
  2.5-cm (1-inch) pieces*
*2 raw mangoes, cut into
  small pieces with the seed
  but discard the kernel*
*1 small cauliflower, cut into
  small florets*
10 green chillies, left whole
*juice of 12 lemons (reserve
  the peel and cut into small
  pieces)*

1 cup chopped fresh ginger
100g (4 oz) chilli powder
*2 tablespoons turmeric
  powder*
4 tablespoons salt or to taste
4 teaspoons mustard seeds
2 tablespoons fenugreek seeds
*300ml (½ pint) mustard or
  sesame oil*

In a large sterilized bowl mix the vegetables, mangoes, lemon peels, ginger, chilli powder, turmeric powder and salt. Cover and leave aside for 24 hours. Dry-roast the mustard and fenugreek seeds and grind them to a fine powder. Heat the oil in a heavy pan and when smoking quickly fry the ground powder. Pour the hot oil over the vegetables and mix well. Store in a warm place for 7–10 days before serving.

Ginger Preserve
Adrak ka Murrabba

This is a nice tangy chutney, and it helps people with intestinal disorders. *Murrabbas* can be made from papaya, *parval*, pineapple, gooseberry, carrot and mango. Use any of these in the same proportion as ginger. All *murrabbas* can be served warm or cold in small quantities with whipped cream as a dessert.

225g (8 oz) fresh ginger
225g (8 oz) sugar
¼ teaspoon citric acid

a pinch salt
½ tablespoon ground saffron strands (optional)

Peel and cut the ginger into thin strips. Mix the sugar and citric acid with 1 cup water and make a one-thread syrup. Add the ginger and salt and bring to the boil. Lower the heat, cover the pan and simmer until you have a thick syrup. Fold in the saffron. Cool and bottle.

Green Tomato Jam
Hara Tamatar Murrabba

*1.3kg (3 lbs) firm green
  tomatoes
550g (1¼ lb) sugar
1 teaspoon grated lemon rind*

*a few drops vanilla
  essence*

Wash and cut the tomatoes into small pieces. In a heavy-bottomed pan add the tomatoes and a little water. Cook until the tomatoes are tender. Mash and extract a thick purée, discarding any seeds and the skin. Place the purée back in the pan and add the sugar. Over a slow heat cook until the sugar has dissolved. When the sugar has dissolved bring the jam to the boil rapidly for 20 minutes or until it reaches setting point. Add the lemon rind and vanilla essence. Pour into sterilized jars and store.

Banana Marmalade
Moaz ka Murrabba

I love eating this delicious marmalade with freshly made toast and whipped cream. We also eat this marmalade hot with freshly made chappatis or *parathas*.

*10 ripe bananas
450g (1 lb) sugar
2 cups water*

*1 lime or lemon
a few drops yellow or
  green food colouring*

Peel and cut the bananas into small pieces. Heat the sugar and water to a one-thread syrup. Cut the lime into thin strips. Add the bananas and lime to the syrup and cook rapidly for about 20 minutes until thick and setting point is reached. Add the food colouring and mix well. Store in airtight jars.

Guava Jelly
Amrud Murrabba

A very popular jelly packed with vitamins.

900g (2 lbs) very ripe guavas *juice of 4 limes or lemons*
1.2 litres (2 pints) water *grated rind ½ a lime or*
900g (2 lbs) sugar *lemon*

Wash the guavas and cut them into small pieces. Cook the guavas in the water until tender and mushy. Pass through a fine sieve and discard the seeds. Place the guava purée in a large heavy-bottomed pan. Add the sugar and bring to the boil. Cook until the jelly starts to set. To test dip a wooden spoon in the jelly, remove, and allow the jelly to stick to the spoon. If the jelly has set it will drop slowly off the spoon and fall into shape. When the jelly is about to set add the lime juice and rind. Transfer to sterilized jars while still hot. Allow to cool before sealing the bottles.

Mango Jam
Aamb Murrabba

2 large medium-ripe *1 cinnamon quill*
mangoes *1 tablespoon honey*
1 cup sugar

Steam the mangoes with their peel for about 15 minutes. When cool enough to handle squeeze out the pulp into a pan. Add the sugar and cinnamon and cook until it reaches setting point. Remove from the heat and cool completely. Add the honey and mix well. Store.

Onion Salad
Kachoomber
Serves 4–6

2 onions, finely chopped
2 firm tomatoes, finely
  chopped
1 green chilli, finely chopped
a handful fresh coriander
  leaves, finely chopped

juice of 1 lemon
a pinch sugar
salt and pepper to taste

Place all the ingredients in a bowl, toss well and serve.

Carrot Salad
Gajjar Kachoomber
Serves 4–6

2 carrots, peeled and grated
  (or white radish)
2 green chillies
a handful coriander leaves,
  finely chopped

juice of 1 lemon
salt and pepper to taste
2 tablespoons oil
1 teaspoon mustard seeds
a few curry leaves

Mix the first five ingredients and keep aside. Heat the oil in a small frying pan and fry the mustard seeds and curry leaves until the mustard seeds begin to crackle. Immediately pour the oil and spices over the carrots and mix well. Chill and serve.

Indian Fruit Salad
Phul Chaat
Serves 4–6

A very appetizing and refreshing fruit salad. We Indians love to combine salt and pepper with fruits, particularly citrus fruits.

2 medium-ripe bananas, cut
    diagonally into slices
2 guavas, quartered
1 small tin mandarin slices,
    drained
1 lime or lemon, sliced
1 naval orange, sliced

1 grapefruit, sliced
salt, pepper and sugar to taste
¼ teaspoon freshly ground
    cumin seeds
½ teaspoon chilli powder (or
    to taste)
a few mint leaves for garnish

Mix all the ingredients and toss well. Chill and serve. Garnish with mint leaves. Serve as a starter, an accompaniment to the main meal or a dessert.

Green Gram Salad
Koshumbri
Serves 4–6

Koshumbri is a very popular accompaniment to any meal but most favoured in the south of India and in the state of Maharashtra.

1 cup green gram (moong)
2 green chillies, seeded and
    finely chopped (leave the
    seeds if you enjoy a hotter
    flavour)
2.5-cm (1-inch) piece fresh
    ginger, chopped

½ cup freshly grated coconut
2 tablespoons oil
½ teaspoon mustard seeds
a pinch asafoetida
a few curry leaves
salt to taste
juice of 1 lemon

Wash and soak the green gram for half an hour and then drain well. Mix the gram with the chillies, ginger and coconut. Heat the oil in a small frying pan and add the mustard seeds, asafoetida and curry leaves and fry until the mustard seeds begin to crackle. Immediately add the oil and the spices to the *dhal*. Add the salt to taste and toss well. Add the lemon juice and toss again. Serve with any meal.

Note: Grated carrot or cucumber can be added to this with coriander leaves as garnish.

Avocado Salad
Makhan ka Chat
Serves 4

I did not realize how plentiful avocados were in the state of Karnataka. In Mysore I ordered this dish not knowing it was avacado as they use the name 'butter fruit'.

2 avocados
½ cup natural yogurt,
  beaten
100g (4 oz) cottage cheese
  with pineapple
1 clove garlic, finely crushed

1 red pepper, finely chopped
salt and pepper to taste
a few lettuce leaves, shredded
1 lime, quartered
paprika and mint leaves for
  garnish

Halve the avocados and remove the stones. Gently scoop out the flesh and cut it into cubes. Immediately fold in the avocado cubes into the yogurt and garlic so that the fruit does not discolour. Add the cheese, red pepper and seasoning. Place some shredded lettuce in the empty avocado shells and top them with the avocado mixture. Garnish with lime, paprika and mint leaves. Chill and serve.

Desserts and
Refreshing Drinks

Besides the recipes for many exotic, traditional sweets, I have included some of my own innovations and some new variations to ancient recipes. Most of the Indian sweets tend to be very rich and sweet. I have tested the recipes with reduced amounts of sugar and found that the dish is just as delicious and does not leave you feeling uncomfortable. We serve the sweets with the main meal and leave the guests to eat it when they please. Most Indian sweets are milk and cheese based and require considerable cooking time. This is partly due to the fact that the climate is usually too hot and when milk is cooked down it lasts longer. Serve Indian sweets in small quantities or allow each diner to help themselves.

Try the delicious non-alcoholic drinks, which you will find at the end of the chapter. Alcoholic drinks are always served on social occasions but I do not agree with this and my guests never feel embarrassed if I have no wine or beer to accompany a meal. We are blessed with so many refreshing drinks like *zeera pani* (cumin water), *nimbu pani* (lime water or, as the British Raj called it, lemonade), mango squash, my favourite tea punch, chilled *lassi* (buttermilk), a popular beverage throughout India, and a variety of sherbets (sweet cold drinks) made from ingredients like tamarind, sandalwood, almonds and even lentils. For an after-dinner drink try our spiced tea and coffee.

Pumpkin Pudding
Kaddu Payasam
Serves 4–6

Payasam is a traditional sweet prepared in the south of India and served in temples for mass feeding. There are several varieties. I have chosen pumpkin *payasam* but you can also try carrots, rice, vermicelli, green gram *(moong dhal)*, sweet potato, *parwal* and beetroot.

450g (1 lb) bottle gourd (white pumpkin)
4 cups milk
3 tablespoons ghee
½ a grated coconut or 1 cup desiccated coconut

3 cardamoms, peeled and ground
¼ cup brown sugar
a few strands saffron
2 tablespoons roasted cashew nuts, coarsely ground

Peel the pumpkin (reserving the peel for the recipe below) and remove the seeds and pith. Grate the pumpkin. Heat the ghee in a large heavy pan and sauté the pumpkin and coconut for 2–3 minutes. Add the milk, cardamom and sugar and simmer until the pumpkin is done. Remove from the heat and fold in the saffron. Serve hot or cold with chopped cashew nuts. Coconut may be substituted with vermicelli and brown sugar with caster sugar.

Pumpkin Peel Snack

The peel is rich in nutritional value and should not be discarded. Try this delicious snack.

Wash the pumpkin peel well and drain. Cut into very thin

julienne strips. Heat enough oil for deep-frying. When hot fry
the pumpkin peel strips until golden brown and crisp.
Sprinkle with salt and chilli powder to taste. Very delicious
with drinks.

Mango Cups
Aamb Piyali
Makes 12

After a heavy meal this makes a very refreshing dessert. Mango
seeds have a lot of flesh on them so do not throw away. Give
them to the children who will enjoy sucking them. But if you
would like to try to grow a mango tree then do not suck them.
It may be an old fairytale but it seems mango seeds that are
sucked will not take root.

6 medium-sized ripe mangoes	*½ cup milk*
1 cup sugar	*2 cardamoms, peeled and crushed*
a pinch saffron	*1 tablespoon honey*

Wash the mangoes and dry them gently with a kitchen towel.
Make a cut right through to the seed around the centre of the
mangoes. Hold the mango on both sides and twist. You will get
one half like a cup and the other half with the seed sticking out
of it. Hold the seed and twist. You will now have two cups.
Scoop out the insides and mash the flesh in a blender or with a
potato masher. Mix all the ingredients in a pan and simmer for
5 minutes. Mix well and refill the mango cups. Chill well and
serve.

Beetroot Pudding
Chugander Halwa
Serves 4—6

This type of pudding is very popular in India and is often served to weak children as a tonic. I have used beetroot but you can also use the same quantity of carrots, bottle gourd or sweet potato.

450g (1 lb) raw beetroot
4 cups milk
3 cups sugar
½ cup butter or margarine

½ teaspoon saffron strands or a few drops of yellow colouring

Peel and grate the beetroot. Place the grated beetroot in a heavy pan and sprinkle in a few drops of water. Cook over a low heat, stirring constantly for about 5 minutes. Gradually add the milk and mix well. Leave to simmer until the milk has reduced to about 2 cups. Then add the sugar and simmer until the sugar has dissolved. Dissolve the saffron strands in a few drops of hot milk or water and add to the mixture. Mix well. Finally, add the butter and stir until the butter has melted and makes the mixture leave the side of the pan. Serve hot or cold. I like to serve it hot with almond flakes and whipped cream.

Corn Starch Pudding
Faluda
Serves 4—6

A very light nutritious pudding. My mother always served this during the summer months as she said it was cooling and would help the brain work better. Alternative flavour suggestions are banana and coffee or almond and green colouring (garnished with mint).

½ cup cornflour
1 cup water
4 cups milk
1 cup sugar

almond essence to taste
rose essence to taste
a few drops red food
colouring

Mix the cornflour with water and pass through a fine sieve. Bring the milk to the boil and remove from the heat. Add the cornflour mixture and return to the heat. Bring to the boil and simmer for 5 minutes. Add the sugar and stir constantly to avoid any scorching at the base of the pan and cook until thick. Remove from the heat and pour half into a wet mould, keeping the remaining half warm. Add almond essence to the milk in the mould. Allow to set. Into the remaining half of the milk mixture add rose essence and a few drops of red colouring to make a shade of pink. Pour over the set mould and allow the second half to set. Chill and serve, garnishing with pink rose petals if in season.

Rice Pudding

Kheer

Serves 4–6

Like *payasam*, *kheer* can be made with a variety of ingredients. Rice *kheer* is the most popular sweet dish in India. It can also be made with sago, vermicelli, sweet potato, pumpkin and fruits like banana, mango and papaya.

1 teaspoon ghee or butter
2.5-cm (1-inch) cinnamon
quill
175g (6 oz) brown sugar
100g (4 oz) coarsely ground
rice

1.2 litres (2 pints) milk
12 cardamoms, shelled and
ground
50g (2 oz) sultanas or raisins
25g (1 oz) almond flakes

In a heavy-bottomed pan melt the ghee or butter and fry the cinnamon and sugar. Add the rice and 1 pint milk. Bring to the boil and then reduce heat and simmer until the rice is nearly done. Add the remaining milk, cardamoms, sultanas and almond flakes. Leave to simmer but keep stirring to prevent the *kheer* sticking to the base of the pan. *Kheer* should have a thick consistency. Serve hot or cold on its own or with *puis* (pages 228–30).

Mango Fool
Aamb ka Mitha
Serves 4–6

Fools can be made from a variety of fruits. Substitute mango with papaya, banana, sapota *(chikkoo)* or custard apple *(sitaphul)*.

400g (14 oz) tinned mango, sliced, drained
2 eggs
100g (4 oz) icing sugar or to taste

100g (4 oz) whipping cream
1 ripe mango, peeled and cut in cubes

Whisk the mango slices until you have a purée. Separate the egg whites and yolk. Add the yolks and icing sugar to the mango purée and mix well. Separately beat the cream and egg whites until stiff and fold them gently into the mango purée. Finally fold in the mango cubes. Chill and serve.

Unleavened Bread Pudding
Mithai Chakoliyan
Serves 4–6

A very popular Hyderabadi dish. The traditional method is very lengthy and complicated and therefore this dish is only prepared on festive occasions. My method is simple using left-over chappatis. In India the chappatis are not roasted on a griddle but dried in the sun before cutting them into small pieces.

6 chappatis (pages 226–8)　　*600ml (1 pint) milk*
oil for deep-frying　　*100g (4 oz) sugar (or to taste)*
2 cloves　　*a few strands saffron soaked*
1 cardamom, bruised　　*in 2 tablespoons warm*
1 cinnamon quill　　*milk*

Cut the chappatis into small pieces. Heat the oil and fry the cloves, cardamom, cinnamon and chappati pieces until they are brown on all sides. Drain and place in another pan. Add the milk and bring to the boil. Reduce heat and allow to simmer until the chappati pieces have absorbed most of the milk. Add the sugar and saffron and continue simmering until the consistency is as thick as a rice pudding. Serve hot decorating with raisins, almond flakes and coarsely ground cardamom seeds or nutmeg. You could also use silver paper and pink rose petals when in season.

Cheese and Yogurt Dessert
Shrikhand
Serves 4—6

Gokulashtmi, the birthday of Lord Krishna, is celebrated with great revel. Earthen pots containing curds (yogurt) and money are suspended from a huge rope on every street corner. Groups of young boys and men climb on each other's shoulders forming a human pyramid and break the pots. This festival is reminiscent of Krishna's childhood pranks. *Shrikhand* is specially prepared on this day as an offering to the lovable Krishna. It is prepared by all the states in India but the Maharashtrans serve it with *puris* which has been their long-standing tradition. The traditional method is very time-consuming so I have adapted it here, but the basic sweet remains the same.

225g (8 oz) low-fat cheese
50g (2 oz) full-fat cream cheese
110ml (4 fl oz) natural yogurt
50—100g (2—4 oz) icing sugar

grated nutmeg to taste
a few strands saffron soaked in a little warm milk
almond flakes to decorate

Chill a large mixing bowl in the refrigerator for 1 hour. Place the cheeses and yogurt in the bowl and whisk with an electric hand whisk. Gradually add the sugar and keep whisking until you have a light and creamy mixture. Add the nutmeg and saffron and mix again. Decorate with almond flakes, chill and serve.

Quick Mango Ice Cream
Serves 4–6

Highlight plain vanilla ice cream with mango.

1 mango
1 small tin mango nectar
(available from Indian
grocers and health-food
shops)

1 small tin condensed milk
a pinch grated nutmeg
1 family block plain vanilla
ice cream

Peel the mango and cut the flesh into small cubes. Place them in 4–6 serving dishes and keep chilled. Beat the mango nectar, condensed milk and grated nutmeg until you have a smooth sauce. To serve place scoops of vanilla ice cream on the mango cubes and then pour some sauce over it.

Spongy Cheese Balls in Syrup
Roshogolla
Serves 4–6

Roshogolla and *sandesh* are two of the most popular Bengali sweets. They are light and easily digestible as no frying is involved. *Sandesh* is considered to be particularly good for children.

225g (8 oz) paneer (page
46)
1 tablespoon flour

1 cup sugar
1 cup water

Knead the *paneer* and flour well until you have a soft dough. Form into small walnut-size balls and keep aside. Make a syrup of sugar and water to a one-thread consistency. While the syrup is still simmering add the *roshogollas* and allow them to swell. Leave them in the syrup and allow them to cool. Serve two or three *roshogollas* per person with a little syrup.

Sandesh

Make the dough as for *roshogollas*. Divide the dough into small balls and flatten them. Place them on a lightly greased tray and steam them until they harden. Chill and steep them in a sugar syrup (made as for *roshogollas*) for 10–15 minutes before serving. You can make different-coloured *sandesh* by dividing the dough and colouring them with food colouring before making them into balls.

A Bengali bride has to prepare herself for several ceremonies which may go on for three to five days and at the beginning or end of each ceremony a sweet is served. When she finally reaches the home of her in-laws her feet are washed in milk and then she is made to watch some milk boil over as a sign that she has brought prosperity with her. Marriages in Bengal are by and large still arranged. The boy's parents first go to the intended bride's house bearing gifts and a large variety of sweets which are decorated on different platters. *Sandesh* and *misthi dhoi* are always included. Bearing these gifts the boy's parents decide on an auspicious time and day for the actual wedding.

Milk Balls in Syrup
Gulab Jamuns
Serves 4–6

This is definitely one of my favourite desserts. The authentic method is time-consuming but when my first son was born I accidentally stumbled on to this method. He was a fussy baby and I had to try several baby milk powders. One day I tried *gulab jamuns* with Ostermilk II and they were just lovely.

350g (12 oz) sugar
600ml (1 pint) water
1 clove
2.5-cm (1-inch) cinnamon
  quill
a few drops rose water
10 tablespoons full cream
  baby milk powder
3 teaspoons self-raising flour

1 teaspoon fine semolina
3 teaspoons ghee or unsalted
  butter
6 cardamoms, peeled and
  seeds ground to a fine
  powder
a little milk to mix
oil for deep-frying

Place the sugar, water, clove and cinnamon in a heavy pan and gently dissolve the sugar. When the sugar has dissolved increase the heat and bring the syrup to the boil. Keep boiling for a few minutes. Add the rose water and set aside.

In a large mixing bowl put the powdered milk, flour, semolina, ghee and ground cardamom. Adding a little milk gradually make a soft dough. Divide the dough into 20 equal portions and roll each one between your palms to make a smooth ball. Heat enough oil for deep-frying and fry a few balls at a time on a low fire until golden brown. At first they will sink to the base but as they fry they become lighter and rise to the surface. Remove with a perforated spoon and transfer to the syrup. When all the balls are fried gently heat the syrup to allow the balls to absorb the syrup and swell. Serve hot or cold.

Dried Apricot Sweet
Akhrot ka Mitha

Serves 4—6

A Muslim dish prepared in addition to other sweets for weddings and auspicious occasions.

450g (1 lb) dried apricots   *900g (2 lb) sugar or to taste*

Place the apricots in a bowl and cover them with warm water. Allow them to soak overnight or until soft, then drain. Now halve them, reserving the seeds, and place in a heavy pan with the sugar and 300ml (½ pint) water. Bring to the boil then reduce the heat and gently simmer until the apricots are soft and mushy and most of the water has evaporated leaving a nice thick juice. While the apricots are cooking break the seeds and remove the kernels. Add these to the apricot mixture while cooking or use them to decorate the dish. Serve hot with custard or thick cream.

Vermicelli Pudding
Shirkhurma

Serves 4—6

This sweet is prepared very early in the morning of Id-ul-Fitr, the feast after the thirty days of Ramazan. When guests arrive to convey their wishes they are welcomed with a dab of *attar* (Indian perfume) and a bowl of this delicious sweet.

6 tablespoons ghee or unsalted butter

1 cup fine vermicelli, broken coarsely

25g (1 oz) almond flakes or slivers

25g (1 oz) pistachio nuts, slivered

25g (1 oz) cudapah nuts (chironji) — optional

50g (2 oz) sultanas or raisins

1.2 litres (2 pints) milk

12 teaspoons sugar or to taste

a few strands saffron soaked in warm milk

Heat the butter in a large heavy pan and sauté the vermicelli until golden brown (if you are using the Italian variety you will need to sauté them longer). Drain and keep aside. Reheat the butter and fry the nuts, raisins, and dates until the raisins swell. Return the vermicelli to the pan and add the milk. Bring to the boil then reduce the heat and allow to simmer until the vermicelli is soft and the milk slightly thick. Add the sugar and saffron and simmer until the sugar dissolves. Serve hot or cold, topping with more slivered nuts if you wish.

Bread Pudding
Dabbal ka Mitha or *Shahi Tukre*
Serves 4–6

I remember with nostalgia the large plates of this lovely pudding which were sent to us from the Nizam's household. I have simplified the method but I promise you that the original taste is the same.

6 thick slices white bread
oil or ghee for deep-frying
100g (4 oz) marzipan
100g (4 oz) almond flakes
50g (2 oz) pistachio nuts,
  slivered
100g (4 oz) sultanas

150ml (5 fl oz) single cream
1.2 litres (2 pints) milk
20 teaspoons sugar or to taste
  (we Indians like this
  pudding very sweet)
a few strands saffron soaked
  in a little warm milk

Remove the crusts from the bread and cut each slice into 4 pieces. Heat enough oil or ghee for deep-frying and fry the bread pieces until golden brown and crisp on both sides. (For those concerned about cholesterol just make toast and then cut the bread.) Drain well and keep aside. Warm the marzipan until soft and then coat one side of the bread with it. Place 2 slices in a heavy pan with the marzipan side on top. Sprinkle the nuts and sultanas. Pour over the cream. Cover with the remaining slices of bread, the marzipan side down. Mix the milk, sugar and saffron and pour over the bread layers evenly. Place on a very low heat and allow to simmer until the bread has absorbed all the milk. Do not disturb the pieces while simmering. If you are worried about the base of the pan burning, place it on a fire-guard. Or you can layer this in a baking dish and bake in a moderate oven until the milk has been absorbed. Serve hot or cold.

Drinks
Sherbets

One of the most effective ways to counteract heat and hot curries is to consume cooling non-alcoholic drinks. I have selected a few, some of which are indigenous to particular communities in India. These drinks are nourishing too. A housewife is often the pivot around which her husband and children revolve, so keep those frazzled nerves and tempers under control with a refreshing drink — and stay cool!

Flavoured Milk
Kachi Lassi
Serves 4

This is a Punjabi favourite, very nutritious and cooling.

4 glasses milk　　　　　　　　*sugar to taste*
100g (4 oz) ground almonds　*4 cardamom seeds, peeled*
a pinch black pepper　　　　　*and powdered*

Bring the milk to the boil and then cool thoroughly. Place the milk and remaining ingredients in a liquidizer and blend for a few minutes. Chill and serve.

Mango Drink
Panna
Serves 4—6

This is a Maharashtran drink.

4 ripe mangoes, peeled	*sugar to taste*
a pinch nutmeg	
a few strands saffron soaked	
in a little warm water	

Boil the mangoes in a little water and when soft and cool enough to handle squeeze out the juice. Mix in the nutmeg, saffron and sugar to taste. Chill and serve. If the juice is very thick you can thin it down with ice cubes or a little chilled water.

Tamarind Squash
Imli Sherbet
Makes approx. 20 drinks

This is a very popular south Indian drink. It will store in a cool place for some considerable time.

225g (8 oz) tamarind	*675g (1½ lb) sugar*
2.4 litres (4 pints) water	

Soak the tamarind in the water until soft. Using your fingers squeeze the tamarind so that the seeds separate. Strain the tamarind juice through a fine sieve into a heavy pan. Bring the tamarind juice to the boil and then simmer for 20 minutes. Add the sugar and bring to the boil again. Reduce heat and simmer for a further 20 minutes. Strain again, cool and bottle. To serve, dilute to taste with chilled or aerated water.

Almond Drink
Badam ka Sherbet
Makes approx. 40 drinks

A very nutritious drink for restoring spent energy.

*900g (2 lb) shelled and
   peeled almonds
6 cups sugar
2 egg whites
12 cardamoms, shelled and
   seeds powdered*

*1.2 litres (2 pints) water
a few drops Kewra essence or
   rose water*

Grind the almonds to a paste and place in a heavy pan. Add the sugar, egg whites and water. Bring to the boil and then reduce the heat and simmer until you have a syrupy consistency. Cool, strain through a fine sieve and mix in the essence. Bottle and store. This will keep for up to 6 months but if you wish to store it longer add 5 or 6 granules of potassium metabisulphate which you can buy from a chemist.

To serve, dilute to taste with chilled water and crushed ice.

Plain albumen water is also a very effective tonic. For this you need 1 egg white per person, 1 cup water, ½ teaspoon glucose and sugar to taste. Beat the egg white until stiff and then mix in the water, glucose and sugar. Strain through a fine sieve, chill and serve with a few drops of lemon juice if you wish.

Mango Squash
Aamb ka Sherbet
Makes approx. 20 drinks

My boys love this drink and they sometimes pour a spoonful of this squash over vanilla ice cream scoops. It stores very well.

*450g (1 lb) mango pulp
  (obtained in tins)
525g (1 lb 3 oz) sugar
450ml (¾ pint) water
15g (½ oz) citric acid*

*5—6 granules potassium
  metabisulphate
a few drops yellow food
  colouring*

In a large heavy pan bring the mango pulp, sugar, water and citric acid to the boil and then simmer until the sugar has dissolved. Cool the juice and strain through a fine sieve. Add the potassium metabisulphate and food colouring. Store in sterilized bottles. To serve, dilute to taste with water and crushed ice.

Spiced Coffee
Masala Coffee
Serves 4—6

We love to spice coffee (and tea) and drink it black and hot during the cool winter months. In India we tend to have air-conditioning in the warm months, but no heating during the winter.

*6 cups water
2.5-cm (1-inch) quill
  cinnamon
4 cardamoms*

*4 cloves
4 coffee bags or ground
  coffee of your choice
sugar to taste*

271

Place the water and spices in a pan and bring to the boil. When the water is aromatic from the spices add the coffee bags and quickly bring to the boil again. If you are using coffee powder tie the coffee in a piece of fine muslin cloth. (If you like your coffee really strong boil for a little longer.) Add sugar to taste and drink hot.

To make spiced tea, follow the same method but use tea bags or tea leaves. A pleasant combination is equal amounts of Assam tea and Earl Grey.

Iced Coffee

Serves 4–6

This is another popular way of serving coffee in India. You will find it on every menu.

600ml (1 pint) strong black coffee, chilled and sweetened to taste
4–6 scoops vanilla ice cream

whipped cream
2 tablespoons grated chocolate or drinking chocolate powder

Chill the coffee thoroughly and pour into 4–6 glasses. Top with helpings of vanilla ice cream and whipped cream. Sprinkle with the grated chocolate and serve at once.

Tea and Fruit Punch
Chai aur Phul ka Sherbet

Serves 12

Serve this delicious punch cold during the summer months and hot during the winter months. If you wish you can add some white wine or brandy to taste.

600ml (1 pint) water
1 cinnamon quill
4 cloves
2½ level teaspoons tea
175g (6 oz) sugar or to taste
150 ml (¼ pint) lemon
  squash

300ml (½ pint) orange
  squash
ice cubes
½ lemon, sliced
50g (2 oz) strawberries, sliced
  (when in season)
a few mint leaves

Bring the water to the boil, pour on to the tea and allow to brew for 3–5 minutes. Stir, strain into a bowl containing the sugar and stir until the sugar has dissolved. Add the lemon and orange squashes. When ready, pour over the ice cubes in a punch bowl and add the sliced fruits and mint leaves.

Cumin Water
Zeera Pani
Serves 4–6

This drink is made throughout India but is mostly favoured by the people of Uttar Pradesh. Serve it with the main meal as an apéritif or a cocktail drink.

6 tablespoons tamarind juice
  (page 60)
2 cups hot water
2.5-cm (1-inch) piece fresh
  ginger, crushed
2 teaspoons fresh ground
  cumin powder

a pinch five-spice powder
sugar to taste
a pinch salt
mint leaves and lemon slices
  for garnish

Mix all the ingredients except the garnish. Strain the juice through a fine sieve and chill thoroughly. Dilute with chilled water if necessary and serve with crushed ice, mint leaves and lemon slices.

Seasoned Buttermilk
Mor
Serves 4–6

6 cups buttermilk
2.5-cm (1-inch) piece fresh
 ginger, finely crushed
2 green chillies, finely
 chopped (seeded for a
 milder flavour)
1 clove garlic, crushed
 (optional)

1 small onion, finely chopped
1 teaspoon cumin powder
a few coriander leaves, finely
 chopped
salt to taste

Beat the buttermilk well and add the remaining ingredients. Chill and serve. (If you do not wish to serve the buttermilk with the whole spices and herbs, tie them in a muslin cloth and steep them in the buttermilk until it is flavoured. Chill and serve.)

Sweet Buttermilk
Mithi Lassi
Serves 4–6

Buttermilk is also delicious when served sweet.

6 glasses buttermilk
sugar to taste
1 teaspoon cumin powder

1 teaspoon fennel powder
salt and pepper to taste

Mix all the ingredients, chill and serve.

Index

Index

277

Index

Index

280

Index

281

Index

Index

Index

Index

Index